DIVORCE BECAME MY SUPERPOWER

Caroline Strawson

Table of Contents

Chapter 1 - Miscarriages & Betrayal

"It's positive!!!" I shouted from the toilet. I had just done a pregnancy test and I was now   expecting our second child. We already had a two-year-old son and we felt the time was now right to have a sibling and ready to cope again with sleepless nights! Harry had silent reflux as a baby, so I was up more or less every hour for at least the first year of his life.

My husband worked for an airline so was away a lot which meant I lived my life pretty much in a permanent state of exhaustion. I had put on 4 stone with my first pregnancy and whilst I had lost some of it, I still was carrying that baby weight that I just didn't seem to have the energy to lose. But today was all about celebrating! A new life had been made and I was very excited.

My husband seemed pleased as he had also said he would like to have two children, so we seemed to be living the ideal family life. We were living in a nice house, a son and a new baby on the way. I wanted to tell my Mum straight away as she was my best friend and I was brimming with excitement.

I was worried how my pregnancy would be though as I felt so poorly when I was pregnant with Harry and seemed to have every pregnancy symptom going including practically being on crutches at the end. I was certainly not one of those women who breezed through pregnancy.

How women say they didn't realise they were pregnant, I do not know! I knew literally straight away. "Let's go around to my Mums and tell her the good news?" I said to my husband. So the three of us went to my parents' house which was only 10 minutes' drive away to tell them the news.

When we arrived at Mums, I literally blurted it out that she was to be a grandma for the third time. They already had a grandson from my middle sister and then Harry and the soon to be new arrival. My Mum was thrilled to bits and was just the best grandma. Both my Mum and Dad were the epitome of what grandparents should be. They absolutely adored Harry and I just knew they would love our new addition too.

I lived in a lovely house with my husband and it was the archetypal family estate. Although I am not particularly religious, we had an amazing vicar and his wife who lived on the estate, who organised so much for the children and to support new parents.

I had a great group of other Mums I had known since Harry was born and we all had babies of similar age and I was going to be the first one in our group to have a second. Should I tell them still being so early on? I had heard a lot of people waited until 12 weeks to tell people, but it didn't even cross my mind that anything would happen as I had no problems with my son, so I told everyone at 7 weeks pregnant.

Everyone was delighted for me as they could see how loved Harry was and I was loving being a Mum. I was trained as a podiatrist and whilst I always still had patients on the side, I had also been working for the same airline as cabin crew with my husband, but when I fell pregnant with Harry I stopped, as I could just not envisage ever being on the other side of the world away from my son especially if something happened to him.

I was thriving being a Mum, I loved it and enjoyed every second of being a parent no matter how tired I was.

Life progressed over the next few weeks and I started to feel sick which was a good sign as I had felt sick with Harry too. Then at 8 weeks pregnant, I went to the toilet and I was bleeding. Panic started to set in. This wasn't just a small bleed, it was a lot! My husband was away in America and I was home alone with Harry.

I called my Mum in tears all worried and asked if she and my Dad come around and bring a pregnancy test. Within 45 minutes they were there, with pregnancy test in hand. I was still bleeding and went to the toilet and took the test. There was still two lines but rather than two bold dark lines, one was noticeably fainter than the other.

My heart sank. I was losing my baby. I just knew it. My baby that I had already decided on how I was going to decorate their room, the day I knew they were to be born, the hopes and dreams that I had for my child. It may have just been a foetus at this stage but to me it was my child that already had a future.

I called my doctor who gave me the number of my local Early Pregnancy Care Unit. I called them up and made an appointment for the next day. They couldn't fit me in that day. I was trying to stay strong in front of my son and my Mum was right by my side offering support as my husband was away.

I called him later that day and told him that it looked like I had miscarried but would not know for definite until I had gone to the unit the next day.

My Mum and Dad took me to the unit the next day, where I had to sit in a room full of people that were still pregnant and inside of me there was still some tiny bit of hope that maybe just maybe there was another reason for my bleed and that maybe everything was ok?! They called my name and into a room I went.

They informed me that as I was only 8 weeks, that they would need to do an internal scan to see what was happening. I took some deep breaths and they did the scan.

Then the nurse uttered those dreaded words "I am so sorry Mrs. Strawson but unfortunately I can't find a heartbeat". The reality hit me, and I realised I had lost my baby. I felt numb and upset and was told to go home and rest as nature was doing the right thing and that as I was bleeding I would need no medical intervention. I went back out to my parents in the waiting room and gave my son a cuddle.

I squeezed him so tight as I needed to feel close to him. I tried to be stoical in thinking how blessed I was in that I had a son already. But I still felt a crushing pain. Was it something I had done wrong? Why was this happening to me? I wasn't even offered any help in coping from the unit other than a leaflet and then sent home.

I went home and called my husband to tell him the devastating news. When he arrived home the next day, he gave me a cuddle and said we can try again. I was in shock as I just had not expected this to happen and it made me realise in that moment that there are so many things that can go wrong with a pregnancy, that if we have a good pregnancy and a healthy baby, how lucky are we?

I had taken all of this for granted with my son as miscarriage was not even something I had thought about, but now I felt bad as I thought of all those women who couldn't have children and I had taken this great gift completely for granted. I would never do that ever again.

The days passed, and I tried to rationalise in my head that miscarriages are far more common than I had even realised. As I told friends that I had miscarried, I was shocked to realise how many other women this had happened to. It seemed such a taboo subject as most people responded with a "must be nature's way" and I even had a few that said, "maybe you can't carry girls".

Although these comments were meant in the nicest of ways, they didn't help, as to me I had lost a baby! My husband seemed to struggle talking about the miscarriage and seemed to go into practical mode by putting a wash on or mowing the lawn seemingly thinking this would help me, but I wanted to try again as 1 in 3 pregnancies can end in miscarriage, so I was trying to resign myself that this was just a blip. That we could try again and move forward.

I really looked at what I was eating and making sure that I was taking the right supplements. I didn't want to risk anything that could jeopardise another pregnancy. My doctor had said to me that there was no reason to wait to try again as they only usually say to wait one cycle as its easier to date the pregnancy but there was no scientific evidence to stop me trying again. I spoke with my husband again and we decided together to try again soon after.

"It's positive" I shouted from the toilet! Relief swept over me. I was pregnant again. The pain of my first miscarriage lessened as 1 in 3 ended in miscarriage so I was just unlucky that time, wasn't I? I felt like a weight had been lifted as I could finally look forward again. I felt more cautious though this time in telling anyone because for a split second, I kept think what if I miscarried again, but I brushed that away from my mind as that wasn't going to happen again. There was no reason for the first, so I would have to be unlucky for that to happen again? At 5 weeks, the sickness kicked in again, and again I thought good, this is a good sign! I told my parents but no one else.

My husband continued to be away a lot with work and I went about all my daily activities with Harry. We had a packed schedule with swimming, music, Mums and tots and toddler gymnastics.

I loved being a Mum and we would have fun every morning and each afternoon, I would try, usually in vain, to get him to nap. Every time I went to the toilet, I realised I would take a deep breath as was worried if I was bleeding but as the weeks started to pass, I started to again imagine their bedroom in our home, what would we be having and picture our life as a family of four and how Harry would like to have a sibling.

Then at 9 weeks, James was away again, and I went to the toilet and there was blood. My heart sank. Please God not again. I blinked again and looked down into the toilet in disbelief. How could this be happening AGAIN! Once I could understand but twice?!

I called my doctor who could tell how upset I was and told me to call the Early Pregnancy Care Unit again and this time, they could fit me in that day. I called my Mum and told her what was happening and as always, she was my emotional support and I dropped Harry off to my parents as James was away and headed down to the unit.

As I sat in the waiting room, I looked around at the faces there. Some were beaming with small bumps and others were upset and pain in their eyes. Surely there should be two separate waiting rooms in the unit? Women like me were sat waiting to be told they had lost their baby whilst being in a room with happy, smiley Mums to be!! I know it's not their fault but talk about rubbing salt in the wound!

"Mrs. Strawson the nurse can see you now." I got up and walked into the all familiar darkened room due to having another scan. I was on my own again as James was away and again because I was 9 weeks pregnant, another internal scan was needed. Deep breaths and a deafening silence whilst I knew she was desperately trying to see if there was a heartbeat. The longer the silence, the more I knew, this was not going to end well. Then that look in my eyes from the nurse of "I am so sorry Mrs. Strawson but there is no heartbeat".

It felt like Groundhog Day. Was this really happening again?! No, it was a dream?! Surely this couldn't happen a second time? But it was. Again, I was given a leaflet and sent home for "nature" to take its course. I went back to my car and sat there and just cried. Tears for my baby that I already loved. Tears for the life that would not be. I am sure people must have looked at me thinking I was crazy as I had mascara all down my face, but I didn't care.

I had lost a second baby and I was devastated. I tried to calm myself down by deep breathing, but I kept breathing like you do when you just can't catch your breath. I started the car and headed back to my Mums to pick Harry up. I had such mixed emotions as on one side I was devastated and on the other I was also truly blessed that I had a son.

What about all those women who kept miscarrying and had no children? As I arrived at my parents, I wiped my face, so I didn't look like a panda as Harry was only two and he didn't understand, and I did not want him to see his Mum crying. I was his rock and his one constant.

As I walked into my parents, the unspoken sentence filled the room and my parents knew without me saying as I scooped Harry in my arms to give him the biggest kiss and cuddle.

They made me a cup of tea, as this was always our family solution to make a cup of tea! Must be our Northern blood. I hadn't even told my husband at this stage as he was still away.

When we arrived back at home, my emotions were all over the place. Anger, guilt, deep emotion all bubbling away inside of me. I called my husband and told him the news. This time I told him I wanted to go to the doctor and get a referral to the hospital as clearly something was wrong.

At this point, I didn't know anyone who had two miscarriages! One was common but two? Now I felt something was wrong?! Maybe with me? Maybe with my husband as he was on a new injection for his reactive arthritis? Was it that? This was when the scientist and my medical background was coming out! I needed answers! I needed a reason as to why? Why was this happening? Why me?

I went into practicality mode now. Once my husband was home, I booked an appointment to see our local doctor determined to ask for a referral to the hospital. Google became my best friend and I was reading everything I possibly could about miscarriages. I needed a reason and an answer.

I joined the Miscarriage Association as this seemed to be the only place where I could get facts and emotional support in a non-judgmental way. Knowing others were going through similar experience made me feel better and that I was not the only one.

Lots of my friends in my baby group were all starting to fall pregnant now, and whilst I was so happy for them, this just highlighted to me that I was a failure as a woman and what was wrong with me?! Every television programme seemed to have pregnant women on, when I went shopping there seemed to be an epidemic of pregnant women everywhere! Of course there wasn't, but to me it just highlighted that I wasn't!

As we explained to the doctor that I had just had my second miscarriage and that we would like a referral, he looked at me and said, "I am sorry, but we only refer to the hospital if you have had three or more miscarriages". I looked at him and said, "You mean I have to go through this a third time before anyone will even take me seriously?" The answer was a big fat yes!

My eyes filled with tears. I couldn't go through that all over again just so I could get to see a specialist. I looked at James and the doctor and asked how much to see privately? The answer was £150 and so I nodded and said, "How do I book?".

The doctor said he would do a letter of referral, and if I called the hospital direct in a few days, I could get the initial appointment. Relief swept over me. At least I felt like I was doing something. Not just waiting! I seemed to have been doing a lot of waiting for time to pass and I needed to feel like I was in control not the other way around. James agreed, and we managed to get an appointment at the end of that week.

When we arrived for our consultant's appointment, I wanted answers. A reason why! I think I wanted him to say;"*this is the reason why, do this or take that and you will have a baby.*"

Sadly, this was not to be. My consultant was very sympathetic and checked me over, weighed me, took my blood pressure, all the usual assessments. He then said that I needed a host of tests including genetic testing and blood tests. So the process began of looking for a reason as to why I kept miscarrying.

The following week, I gave blood and awaited the results. Could there be an answer as to why this was happening? I called my doctor the next day as my results were in. What was wrong with me? The answer was not what I wanted to hear. Nothing was wrong with me!

There was no reason why I was having miscarriages and in fact 50% of miscarriages are unexplained and no known reason is found! This was worse for me than finding out that something was wrong because it meant trying again wondering if I would have another miscarriage. James went into practicality mode again as he rarely showed emotion and seemed unsure how to console me. I didn't realise that whilst all this was going on, we were becoming even more emotionally distant from each other.

However, we both wanted a sibling for Harry, so we decided to try again. I went on eBay and bought one hundred cheap pregnancy sticks as realised that the moment one of the lines on the pregnancy stick started to go faint in the early stages of pregnancy, that this was a sign for me that I was miscarrying. I saw my specialist and he gave me progesterone pessaries that he said may help me hold onto my pregnancy.

Even just feeling like I was trying something made me feel better. I was reading everything I could about miscarriages and was becoming obsessed with getting pregnant. More friends were becoming pregnant and a constant reminder that I was not! It seemed I had no problem getting pregnant because that month I fell pregnant again for the third time.

This time I felt positive, albeit scared too. Every single time I went to the toilet I did a pregnancy test literally just to reassure myself. The lines were strong, the sickness was there, was this going to be third time lucky?

At 8 weeks, my consultant booked me in for an early scan. I still wasn't bleeding, could this be the pregnancy that would give Harry a sibling? James and I went to our appointment for the scan and this time I was one of the smiling Mum's in the waiting room. I was there and still pregnant! As they called us into the all familiar room, the memories came flooding back.

What if there was no heartbeat again? As it was still only 8 weeks, an internal scan had to be done. This time the nurse smiled and said "Look, there is the heartbeat!". Tears streamed down my face and I grabbed James hand. This was our baby! This was our brother or sister for Harry. Our family could now be complete!

As the weeks went on, I still felt sick and I was still using a pregnancy stick every time I went to the toilet, but my worry was lessening. I was fast approaching the 12-week mark and my next scan was booked for 13 weeks. As we arrived at the Antenatal Unit it was so busy! Expectant Mums everywhere!

We had brought Harry with us this time to take into the scan, so he could feel part of it. We were all very excited. We were going to see our baby. My consultant called me in initially on my own just to check me over before we would call in James and Harry.

I walked in beaming and all excited. Chattering away to my consultant telling him proudly how sick I was still feeling. I pulled up my top and he put the icy cool jelly on my tummy and put the probe on my tummy. He started moving it around and pressing firmly.

The silence was deafening and going on far too long. My heart started pounding and my consultant quietly said, "How many weeks should you be?" I looked at him and quietly replied "13 weeks." He put the probe down and said those fatal words "I am so sorry Caroline, but your baby has stopped growing at 9 weeks and there is no heartbeat."

Had I just heard that correctly? My baby had died? I had been

15

carrying a dead baby inside me for 4 weeks? I looked at him and couldn't even cry. I felt numb. I said I need to go to the toilet and I got up and walked across the hall looking down the hallway at where Harry was happily playing with my husband. James looked up at me and I just shook my head and disappeared into the toilet.

How could this be happening a third time? Luckily Harry was still a bit too young to take it all in and the fact he was there meant I had to hold it together. My consultant took me into his room and explained that as my body had not naturally expelled the baby, I would need to book into the hospital to have what is called a D&C.

There were no available appointments for 4 days. I looked at him and said, "You mean I have to walk around for 4 days knowing I am carrying my dead baby?". He replied with a "Yes".

I was shocked about this and have since found out that this is a common occurrence due to staff shortages. I went to join James and Harry and we went back home. I was numb and in shock. James seemed to not know what to say to me, so he just didn't say anything. Harry was the light in this dark moment, playing and smiling. Thank goodness we had him.

Four days later my Mum came with me to the hospital for my appointment. As I lay in the bed, I realised that I was literally on a conveyor belt of women who were having either abortions or D&C's due to miscarriage. This became apparent when I went into the operating theatre and clearly the nurse had not read my medical notes or the reasons why I was there as she tried to make small talk and said to me, "Is it just the two kids you have?"

I looked at her with a steely gaze and said "No, just the one. This would have been my second". She must've realised her faux pas as the next moment I was being anaesthetised and then back on the ward with my Mum sat next to me. I have never felt so numb. I had so many emotions going around in my head. One half of me was saying I want to try again and the other was saying I can't ever go through that again.

When I arrived back home, we hardly spoke about what had happened. I felt alone and focused on my son. I had such mixed emotions as I was blessed that I had Harry, but I desperately wanted a brother or sister for him. The doctor had advised me that we could try again whenever I felt ready. I was becoming almost obsessed by this stage. I am not a quitter but maybe a sibling for Harry was not meant to be?

We tried again as I almost needed to know I could get pregnant again but again at eight weeks, I miscarried for the fourth time. James and I discussed what to do after the fourth miscarriage and I said I wanted to try one last time. If I miscarried again, I said I could not put myself through that again. Someone suggested acupuncture so I started seeing a local acupuncturist specialising in fertility.

As usual I fell pregnant the first time we tried and this time, I felt different. I was scared but it was like this feeling inside of me that I knew I would be ok and so would our baby. The 8-week scan came, and all was fine, the 12-week scan came, and all was fine. My consultant then informed me that my risk of miscarrying now was simply the same as everyone else, so much lower.

I bought my own Doppler heartbeat monitor and my morning and evening routine became finding my baby's heartbeat to reassure me each day. I was a sick as a dog and felt dreadful but inside I was ecstatic. When it came to my 20-week scan, we decided to find out the sex and we were told we were having a daughter. I cried! Our perfect little family would be complete. Harry would have a beautiful baby sister.

My world seemed complete. Life was good, and all the heartache of my miscarriages were fading because I had a new focus. I would never forget these four babies that should have been, but I felt truly blessed that I was about to complete our little family.

When James was away on his trips, I really struggled as I just felt so tired and sick, but nothing could dampen my happiness. One night when James was home from one of his trips, I had cooked them both tea. I was still not eating and was losing weight in my pregnancy but just couldn't face eating.

They were both sat down having their tea, when my husband's mobile phone started to ring in his coat pocket that was hanging in our downstairs toilet. As I was nearest, I simply went to get it to give to my husband, but he shot up, grabbed it out of my hand and started pressing the buttons.

It all seemed a bit strange? He informed me he had inadvertently locked his phone. Suddenly, I felt my heart beating faster and my gut was telling me something was not right? I said to him, "Go back to eating your tea and I will call the mobile phone company and get unlocked, after all the phone was in my name".

James seemed to get angry at me and told me not to and the more he said that, the more compelled I felt to do it. I took the phone and went into our study and called the phone company and within minutes I unlocked the phone.

There was a voicemail message left so I listened to it on my own in the study. It was an American woman saying hi to her gorgeous Englishman. She was asking if he was having a lovely weekend with his son Harry and that she was missing him. My heart sank. Could I be hearing this correctly? I walked out of the study shaking. James got up from the table and came into the hallway. I put the phone to his ear and said who is this? I told him he needed to get out of our house. He looked me in the eye and almost shouted, "I don't know what you are talking about!".

I made him listen to the voicemail whilst I clung to the phone. When he finished listening, he looked me direct in the eye and said, "It's a mistake, I don't know who that was, and it was a coincidence!". He said it so convincingly. Was I crazy? I called my Mum and Dad as felt so confused. They both came around and I made them listen to the message. They looked at James and said, "It doesn't look good, does it James?".

He looked them both in the eye and again said it was a mistake, a coincidence and that he did not know who this woman was, even though she mentioned our son's name. He still denied it and said it was a coincidence. He was so convincing. I started to even doubt myself? The number was from Chicago, so I went and checked my husband's rosters and he had done more than a usual number of trips there recently.

I even called the number and a woman answered and I asked her why she had called this number. She informed me it was a mistake and she had dialled the wrong number. I felt so confused. this was my husband, I was pregnant with our miracle baby? What was going on? I needed to sleep on it and process it all.

The next morning when I got up, I asked for my husband's crew card. This was a credit card that the airline gave him to withdraw money each trip and I wanted to see what he had been spending. He gave me his wallet freely and seemed very relaxed still maintaining it was all a big mistake! I went into our study to logon and check. I couldn't access the account as there seemed a glitch in the system, but I found a business card in my husband's wallet of a motel based in Chicago.

Why did he have a motel business card when you get given hotel accommodation from the airline? On the back of the business card was a reservation number. My heart was pounding, and I felt sick. What was happening in my little world?

I called the motels' reservation number and said I was double checking a reservation and gave the reservation number that was on the back of the business card. I pretended to be Mr. Strawson's PA! The man in reservations informed that the reservation had been cancelled the week before and this was when my husband's trip to Chicago had been changed as I was poorly.

I hung up and just sat there for what seemed like an eternity. I slowly got up and stood in the doorway of the lounge looking at my husband with tears running down my face and said to him, "Are you still going to deny this?" I could tell that he was thinking in that split second, can I still deny this, or has it now gone too far?

Finally, he admitted that he had been having an affair with an American woman for six months. My heart sank, and I could barely breathe! I was six months pregnant, we had a son together and a home. My husband started crying begging me to forgive him. Telling me he felt responsible for my miscarriages and this was his release and someone to talk to.

I had always said whilst growing up that if anyone ever cheated on me that would be it. I would be off, but we had a life together. Maybe this was my fault? Maybe if I hadn't had the miscarriages, he wouldn't have had the affair? He did seem very sorry and was promising me that he would never do this again.

Over the next few days, we talked, I cried, and we decided that we would stay together and make it work. I even ended up being the one comforting my husband as he felt guilty and upset. But inside I felt numb and that something inside of me had died, but I had my son and my unborn daughter to think about and I did not want to rip my family apart for just one mistake.

So, life continued and in three months, I gave birth to our beautiful daughter "Grace". I started suffering with post-natal depression and my midwife had told me I was high risk due to what had happened with the affair. One minute I would be happy and the next I would be angry. One evening, James and I were sat at the kitchen table and I was trying to explain how I was feeling but James just couldn't seem to understand.

I was trying to explain how insecure I felt due to his affair and as he was talking, he accidentally called Grace by his mistress's daughters name. My blood ran cold. I looked at him right in the eye and said, "Don't you ever call our daughter by any other name ever again".

It's funny because when it came to me, I seemed to have little strength but when it came to my children, my mother's instinct kicked in. How dare he call our daughter another name. She did not deserve that, she was our miracle baby.

So, life just kind of meandered on. We never really discussed this ever again and we just started trying to be a family again and move forward.

Chapter 2 - Losing My Mother

After Grace was born, days turned into weeks and weeks into months. When James was away, I felt on edge because if he had cheated on me before, then surely, he could do it again?

Every time I asked what he was doing when he was away, he would get angry at me for questioning him. I felt like I wanted to sit down and really talk about everything so that it was all out in the open because I still felt like he wasn't sorry. There was a niggling feeling inside of me.

Did he feel that because he had cried and said sorry that it had made it all OK? I said to him that if he had murdered someone, you wouldn't just say sorry and then everything would be OK, you would try and show remorse and apologise and want to make it right with the other person. I just felt like he thought it was all forgotten, but he had hurt me so much to the core and I had always said, if anyone had ever cheated on me, I would dump them and here I was compromising all my own values and boundaries.

When I was younger, cheating was always up there on my list of deal breakers. If someone cheats, there is something fundamentally wrong in your relationship and I kept thinking surely James should be trying much harder to reassure me?

The one thing that was really keeping me going was my children. I was born to be a Mum. I loved it and had a fabulous routine going with them both, of lots of activities in the morning like swimming, music, Mums and tots' groups and then in the afternoon, I would try and get them to nap. 'Try' being the operative word. Grace was suffering with a condition called silent reflux. Harry had also had this and it meant their feeding was painful for them and lots of squirming and wriggling.

Grace was waking eight to ten times a night and I was exhausted. I was on medication for my post-natal depression and this seemed to be helping me, but I felt like a big chunk of my life had been shattered. Through all of this, my Mum was my rock. We had always had the most amazing relationship and she was always my cheerleader in life. If anything was ever worrying me, she would always be my first port of call. I would even try and call her on the phone sometimes and it would be engaged because she would be calling me.

She was a natural Mum and gave me cuddles when I needed, praise and advice if asked for and was just my one constant. Don't get me wrong, I love my Dad but the bond between my Mum and I was unshakeable. She was quite literally my world. Growing up, my Mum was always there for my sisters and me. We had lived in Papua New Guinea when I was three for two years and we all had a real passion for travel in our family.

I always remember birthdays and Christmas being huge in our house as my Mum would just make each one so memorable and we always had a birthday party and a birthday cake. She was such a big kid and both us loved to make an effort at birthdays and Christmas, decorating the room and getting a nice birthday cake with candles.

The whole nine yards. We never had much money growing

up, but I never felt like I missed out. Our house was filled with love and my Mum was the matriarch at the head of it. She had left school at sixteen as my grandma was a single Mum, so my Mum needed to work to help support the house. Now, my Mum was a clever woman but never had the opportunity for university and this was something that she was passionate about for me and my sisters.

Both Mum and Dad doted on Harry and Grace and thrived on being grandparents. My middle sister also had a son, but they lived over in the USA, so they didn't see them as much, plus the fact we lived 10 minutes from my parents was great. Harry and Grace loved being with my parents and my Mum just seemed to have so much time to sit and chat to Harry whilst she was cuddling Grace.

Harry had an amazing relationship with my Mum and Harry always used to strip off his clothes everywhere and back his bare bottom into my Mum, and my Mum would squeal with laughter and tell him how naughty he was! It was such a pleasure watching this special bond relationship. She would sit and tell them story after story and both my children adore books now too.

I grew up loving books from my parents and that had now passed down the generations. Time stood still for my Mum whenever we saw her with Harry and Grace. Her face lit up whenever we were with her and my Dad. My Mum suffered with severe rheumatoid arthritis and even had titanium rods in her wrist. She was in constant pain daily, but I never heard her moan once. Her mobility was limited and even simple daily tasks like turning the tap on were difficult for her. She smoked, and this was really the only thing we ever really disagreed on.

I am a huge anti smoker and it always worried me about my Mum and her smoking, but she said she enjoyed it and was her only vice and that if she stopped, she said, the stress would kill her! I had spoken in depth to my Mum about what happened with James and she told me that I would know when the time was right if I needed to leave, and that she would be there to support me whatever or whenever that decision was to be made. She always made me feel better. She was my soft place to fall, my security and my anchor in life. Being in her arms just made me feel safe. Safe and secure and that I always knew I had an anchor in the world.

Saturday 29th March 2009 started as any normal day would. I got up with the kids and had made
them breakfast. James was on a flight that day to Boston, so he had left early. I took the kids to   the park as it was a beautiful sunny day and Harry had raced around like he always did. He had so much energy and just never seemed to stop.

When we got home, I put Grace to bed and Harry and I sat down and started watching The Prince of Egypt cuddled up on the settee. I loved just being with my children as knew that they were growing up so fast and I wanted to savour every moment. About half an hour into the film, I saw my Dad walk past my lounge window. He looked hunched and pinched lipped and I thought something had happened with my gran.

My grandma, my Mum's Mum, was still alive and in a home near us but she was in her early nineties and we all wondered how much longer she had left. My Dad walked in through my front door as he never knocked, and I got up and went into the hall to greet him. Harry followed me and was by my side.

My Dad looked pale and grey and looked into my eyes and said with a shaky voice "It's your Mum". I asked, "What do you mean?" My Dad looked me in the eyes and simply uttered two words that I will never ever forget, "She's dead". What? What did he just say? Dead? Surely that wasn't right? I asked my Dad again, "She's what?". "Dead", my Dad uttered with a

25

quiet voice.

At this point Harry was looking at me for my reaction and my Dad was looking at me in complete shock. I needed to take action and I needed to take control. I had to be strong because what was my alternative with Harry and my Dad stood looking at me? I asked my Dad if he had told either of my sisters and he hadn't. I asked how and when and wanted to know all the details of what had happened.

My Mum had woken that morning early in severe back pain. Now my Mum never moans about pain because she is in constant pain, but this was different this time, she knew something wasn't right but didn't want to make a fuss. She tried taking some painkillers as she just thought maybe it was a bad flare up of her arthritis, but it started to get worse.

My Dad called the paramedics and they came out to my Mum. She explained her symptoms and they seemed to think it could possibly be kidney stones with all the symptoms she was showing. My Mum and Dad seemed appeased with this hence why they did not call me as it seemed to all make sense.

They took my Mum to the hospital, but the pain was getting worse. She was starting to get more and more agitated at the hospital. At about 11am, my Mum started screaming in pain as she just couldn't cope anymore, and they gave her some morphine. This seemed to calm her down and at this stage, and both my parents believed that it was still kidney stones, so again they didn't call me even though I was 15 minutes from the hospital as they knew James was away and I was home with Harry and Grace and they didn't want to alarm me.

My Mum and Dad started chatting about their most recent holiday to Madeira. This was one of their favourite places. They both loved to travel but due to my Mum's arthritis, they travelled less than when they were younger. They were reminiscing about sitting in their favourite cafe, having coffee together and watching the world go by. I got my thirst for travel from them.

As they were laughing and reminiscing, a new doctor came into the room. A face they had not seen before. It was the chief vascular surgeon of the hospital. He looked at both my parents with a serious stare and started to explain that my Mum was in a very serious condition.

She had an aneurysm in her aorta and it had ruptured and needed operating on immediately. The operation was risky with no guarantees and the recovery would be slow. As they were explaining all of this, my Mum fell backwards into her bed and started to arrest. The doctors and nurses were shouting at each other and the crash cart came out and they started working on my Mum to revive her. They used the defibrillator and they kept trying, all with my Dad looking on in disbelief. They tried for over 20 minutes to try and revive her. It was to no avail.

My Mum had died. My beautiful, precious, amazing Mum had passed away at just 67 years of age on the 28th March 2009 at 1.10pm. My Dad was in shock and the hospital allowed him to walk out and leave without even asking him if he needed anyone to be called. So, my Dad got in his car from seeing my Mum die before his eyes and drove straight to me.

I was now in automatic mode. I sat my Dad down and got toys out for Harry and called both of my sisters. My eldest sister got in her car and said she was on her way to us. She lived just over an hour away and my middle sister who lived in the USA didn't answer the phone initially as it was in the middle of the night.

A picture was starting to build about how the hospital had

thought it was kidney stones and then as the morning progressed and she had an ultrasound, the junior A and E doctor suspected a ruptured aneurysm but because it was a Saturday, did not want to call out the chief vascular surgeon unless it was 100%.

I felt numb inside and contacted the airline of my husband and they said that as soon as he landed in Boston, they would put him straight on next available flight home which was to be the Sunday morning. I asked my Dad if I could go and see my Mum and he gave me the number of the hospital. I had this urge that I needed to see her, and this almost became an obsession over the next 24 hours.

I needed to see my Mum. I had to see her in person. I needed to see with my own eyes that she was gone because otherwise maybe just maybe this was just a bad dream?

My sister arrived not long after and we both hugged and cried but I think we were all just in shock. My Mum, my rock, my best friend, was no longer alive. How could this be? My Dad and my sister went back to my Dad's later that day leaving me with Grace and Harry. I kept hugging them and Harry kept asking what had happened. I told him that Grandma had gone to heaven to be with the angels, but she was looking down on us and always would be.

I don't think Harry understood at this point which was a good thing because I am not sure how I would have coped if he started crying. I was really struggling to cry because I felt so scared that if I started, I wouldn't stop. I put them both to bed that night and as I got into bed, the first tear started and then literally I couldn't stop. I just couldn't process the fact that my Mum had died.

I was never, ever going to see her again. I was never, ever going to feel her arms around me again, how was I going to survive? She was my rock. I lay face down in the pillow sobbing for what seemed like an eternity. I cried until I literally had no more tears that could come out. I must've fallen asleep from sheer exhaustion in a haze of sadness.

When I woke up the next morning, James arrived back to our home. He came in and took over the care of Grace and Harry and I went out for a run. I needed to release this pent-up tension that was building in me. I ran around our country park as fast as I could until I had no more energy to run. I found a bench in the park and just simply sat and started to cry.

I was almost howling with tears and sadness and I was sure people must've thought I was mad! I went back to the house and called the hospital. I needed to see my Mum. They told me that I could have an appointment at 4pm that day to go and visit her in the hospital's morgue. I spent the rest of the day on edge, as if this was all a dream. Surely it wasn't really happening? By this time, I had spoken to my sister in the USA and she was in the process of booking a flight back home.

My Dad and my eldest sister did not want to go and see my Mum. Just me. I do not know why but the urge that I needed to see her was so great that it took my breath away. I became obsessed with finding a pendant of my Mums at their house as I needed to feel I had something of hers. My heart was literally aching like it was breaking. At 3.30pm, I headed over to the hospital and found a map and started to walk to the morgue.

There were people all around and yet I felt like I was having an out of body experience. As I entered the morgue, there was two people waiting for me. They ushered me into the room where my Mum was and then left me alone with her. I looked at my beautiful Mum lying there with a big purple velvet cover over her body. I touched her face. It felt like stone. Riga mortis had set in. I could hear a wheezing sound almost like she was still breathing, and I was later to find out that this sound was normal in aftermath of death. I could see where they had cut her open in her chest in a big Y for the post mortem.

Was this real? Was this my Mum? My Mum who was my world, my Mum who was my best friend? I held her hand in mine and started to talk to her. Telling her how much I loved her and always would. I must've been in there for over 20 minutes simply touching her and talking to her. I had my mobile phone with me and almost wanted to take a picture. A picture to prove she was dead as my head was still not registering. It didn't seem appropriate though, so I never did.

I didn't want to leave her. I wanted to stay with my Mum. Tears rolled down my cheeks but this time there was no sound. It was real, this was my Mum. My Mum was dead. I would never ever look into my Mums' eyes again. I would never feel my Mums' arms wrapped around me again. My children would grow up without a grandma. How could this have happened?

The next few weeks were a blur and funeral arrangements were made. I went into coping mode as I had my children and needed to look after them and my father who was in shock. I didn't have time to grieve. Maybe if I didn't grieve, then I could pretend that it hadn't happened? Before the funeral, the funeral director said he needed to take off my Mum's rings and would anyone in the family like to be the one to do it. Immediately I said me!

No one else wanted to see my Mum like that but I felt such a strong need to go and see her as I just didn't want to be apart from her. So, I drove to the funnel parlour and walked in to see my Mum for what would be the final time. The room was lit with candles and my Mum was lying in her coffin. We had decided to bury her in her dressing gown as it was a family tradition that we never got dressed before lunch as we were too busy chatting and having cups of tea.

She looked so beautiful and peaceful. I touched her hand and it had softened now. It was almost as if she could just be fast asleep. If only. If only this was just a bad dream and not happening. I gently took all Mum's rings off. Her wedding ring and engagement ring. I kissed her on the forehead and whispered, "Rest in Peace my beautiful Mum and you will always be in my heart."

I turned around and it was one of the hardest things I have ever had to do to walk out of that room, because in that moment I could simply just pretend she was asleep, but the reality was she was dead and never, ever was I going to see her again.

My Mum's funeral was beautiful and both myself and my two sisters all stood and spoke some words. We wanted to do my Mum proud. She was so passionate about her three girls and growing up always wanted us to all get a degree, so we would always have that to fall back on if we ever needed to.

A few weeks after my Mum's funeral, I went to see the vascular surgeon at the hospital as I had questions that needed answering about the care my Mum had, and being in the medical profession I couldn't rest until I had them. The surgeon was a wonderful and kind man and was so giving with his time to talk to me about my Mum.

He explained that mistakes had been made but that more than likely the result would have been the same. I had done my own research about abdominal aortic aneurysms (AAA's) and once ruptured, highly unlikely that anyone survives. They call this condition the ticking time bomb as most people do not even know they have it unless found through another surgical

31

procedure. I also wanted to ask him as I had read that AAA's were hereditary and this worried me for my own children. He asked me if I was a smoker or had ever smoked and I had never. He informed me that he had never seen an AAA in a non-smoker in all his years of practice and this reassured me and both of my sisters when I informed them.

So, life just kind of went on. James and I were becoming more and more distant. He would go away on his trips and I would still call now and again and often never get a reply. I felt angry a lot of the time. Angry that I had lost my Mum and angry that I felt like James was not making any effort in our marriage. We were just really living under the same roof and I felt I was getting very little emotional support and was just focusing on being a Mum to Harry and Grace.

In the year following my Mum's death, my Dad decided to get both of his knees replaced. I think this was his way of doing "something" to take his mind of losing my Mum, but this meant that I had to take him to hospital and help with his recovery.

This meant, I had no time to grieve as I was caring for my Dad and my two children. Over that year, James' behaviour was starting to become erratic and he was getting more snappy. I decided that I would try and get some grief counselling as I really felt I had not dealt at all with losing my Mum as I couldn't cry about it because quite simply, I had put it all in a box in my head and locked it tight.

I booked an appointment and went along. I was in a room with this lovely lady, but I was not ready. I came away feeling so angry that I thought I can't go back. I needed to keep focused as I had two children relying upon me and my marriage was on the rocks.

I couldn't factor in more anger and I felt again that if I opened the floodgates, I just wouldn't be able to stop. I needed to be ready and feel stronger in myself before I visited that box!

James just seemed so distant all the time and every time I tried to make an effort or try to explain how I was feeling, it always ended in an argument and I always felt like I was in the wrong for trying to bring it up.

He would then be off on a flight somewhere and the cycle would just keep continuing.

Chapter 3 - I Think I've Killed Someone?

As the days progressed, my focus became more and more on my children. I loved being a Mum and every morning I had something planned with the kids and then in the afternoon, I tried to get them to nap. Harry was due to start nursery at age three and I had put his name down for an amazing preschool local to me that would start in the mornings from September.

Education was important to me and I wanted to be with my children until they started school, but I recognised that it would also do Harry good for the year that preceded school, for him to get used to being away from me and socialising for a few hours each day. It was a wonderful nursery and Harry was such an active child, that this nursery had so much outdoor space, that I knew he would love it.

When he started, Grace was still a baby and each day, I would drop him off. He never cried but I could tell how anxious he was. I am not sure who struggled more, myself or Harry being apart. I had become so close to my children, that they were becoming the only feeling of self-worth that I had.

James was away for days at a time and I would wonder what he was doing on the trips. Some trips, I was so busy, I gave little thought to it but sometimes, I would be sick with worry what he was doing. I would often try and call him at night wherever he was just to see if he answered. Sometimes he did but the times that he didn't, I started to imagine all kinds of scenarios.

You see, I had worked for the airline myself before I was pregnant with Harry, so I knew exactly what could happen on these trips when people were away from home. Every trip would be a new crew and potentially an opportunity for James to meet someone.

James had been married before to another cabin crew member. As far as I knew at this stage, this had ended in divorce because he had told me that he had married too young. This made sense to me as she was older than him and wanted to settle down, whereas James was still in his early twenties so all that made sense to me and I could understand why their marriage had not worked out.

I will be honest though, that when I first met James and heard he had been married before, it really put me off. I had never envisaged myself being a second wife as was just my conception of it. I suppose I was an old romantic really. I had grown up with all the Ladybird books of fairy tales with Prince Charming and Happily Ever Afters.

Being a second wife didn't quite fit with my life plan! In fact, when I first met James on a flight, I was trying to fix him up with my friend. I thought he was asking me lots of questions about being single and so naively, I was telling him all about my friend. Little did I know, he was chatting me up and had his sights firmly set on me.

When James was home, he was a good Dad at this time and would come with me when I took James to preschool and Grace to her activities. She was still so young, but I loved going to all of them. James and I attended these sessions together, but it never felt like we were together. I suppose I got so busy as much as I could, so it would stop me focusing too much on our relationship.

James was sleeping in another room and Grace was sleeping with me. I think this was my security as I certainly was not ready to be in the same bedroom as James. I still felt so hurt that he could cheat on me when I was pregnant. Having had four miscarriages, I knew how hard it was to go through that and the Miscarriage Association were a godsend to me.

I would read all the literature that they had, and I was on their forums chatting with other women who had been through similar experiences. I felt so blessed that I had two healthy children that I wanted to give something back, so I trained to become a Miscarriage Association Counsellor, so I could help others going through this.

One day, I got a call from the association asking me if I would be interested in talking to a national magazine who wanted to do a story on recurrent miscarriages. I said yes as always, a big believer in helping others in any way I can, and it had been such a tough experience for me. So, I had a phone interview with a lady who asked me all about my miscarriages.

I am not sure why, but it was like a floodgate had been opened and I found myself telling her all about the four miscarriages and my husband's affair. I am not sure whether it was conscious or unconscious, but it felt good talking to someone about it. As I was telling her about the affair, I found myself giving reasons and excuses as to why it had happened as I said James was probably lonely as I was sick in my pregnancy and it had been a big emotional rollercoaster going through the miscarriages.

She asked if I minded if the angle of the story changed to

include how miscarriages can affect a relationship and could she interview James. I said I would ask him. When I asked James, I could tell he was uncomfortable with this and I almost felt a twinge of revenge inside of me. Ha! You put me through what you did, so the least you can do is admit it and talk to this lady.

He did agree to talk to her and she interviewed him over the phone too. When the magazine article came out, I didn't quite realise the angle it would have but the headline of "4 Miscarriages, a cheating husband and a miracle baby" kind of said it all!

In fact, if you google my name, this is one of the very first items that come up of the actual magazine article. When I saw it, something inside me felt like I had got my own back a bit as it must've been very uncomfortable for James, but I suppose what could he say as it was only the truth that was written and even quoting what he had said too.

Over the coming weeks and months, life with James was becoming more and more distant. I kept trying to talk to him because I still felt so insecure and wanted reassurance. I felt fat and ugly as I had put weight on after having Grace and was really struggling to lose it as I just felt tired and emotionally drained all the time.

For half my life, I felt like a single Mum when James was away and then when he would come back, I would try and make an effort as I really wanted our marriage to work and would try so hard to talk and initiate some emotion. It always ended either in a row or me crying, feeling really low and unloved.

I was all knotted inside because I had always been so strong and ambitious when we met, and I even remember having a conversation with James saying that as we were getting more serious, that if he ever cheated on me, that would be it. I had always had very strong views on this and had never been cheated on as I always ended relationships if they hadn't felt right. James knew this and so I felt like I was in battle with myself because my head was saying leave, but my heart was saying, we are married, we have a family, we have a life together, but I felt so betrayed especially as I was pregnant at the time! This to me was the ultimate betrayal.

My self-esteem started to dwindle and decline because I felt stuck. On one hand, I loved my children and I suppose in some way, I must've loved James still, but I just felt so cheated and betrayed. How could he have treated me like that? But again, I would make excuses so that it fitted in a box in my head. I was missing my Mum so much and she was always the one I would talk to about situations like this, but I couldn't do that. I had lost my Mum and felt like I was losing my husband.

James would periodically show me some love and emotion and I would think, maybe things will work out? Maybe it was a one off and just a mistake? It happens right? I mean, it was a tough time in our life and four miscarriages is hard for anybody and any marriage? I always seemed to be able to find a reason not to leave. My parents had been married over forty years when my Mum died and marriage to me was sacrosanct. I got married for life. It was not a game to me and I took my vows very seriously. Through sickness and health.

Due to James flying and no routine to his schedule, I found socialising with friends very difficult. I remember on one occasion, my baby group had arranged a night out at a local pub and for once I thought I could go as James was at home, so I informed my friend who had organised it that I could finally go to one. She informed me that I wasn't invited.

This was so deeply upsetting to me as I was already feeling more and more isolated due to James' job. To be penalised because I couldn't go out like they all could because of my husband's job hurt me so deeply as I felt like I had done something wrong.

How could she be so cruel? What had I done wrong other than be a Mum to Harry and Grace and that was why I couldn't go out to the other social meet ups. This made me feel even worse as I questioned if something was wrong with me?

My husband had cheated, and I was barely going out other than to drop Harry off at preschool and do Grace's morning activities. My life was revolving around my children. My baby group seemed to be meeting in the evenings and I struggled with that because of James' job. Again, I started to feel isolated.

I started to comfort eat and put on weight. I felt very sorry for myself. Why was all this happening to me? I was a good person and had always been brought up to treat people the way you want to be treated, but it seemed that my husband and a few friends felt it ok to treat me in a different way?

I lived on an estate and everyone knew what James had done and it must have been a great talking point for people to have a good gossip about, but this was my life too. I didn't know anyone else that had a husband who had cheated or who had lost their Mum and certainly not where both had happened!

So why were people so uncaring and cruel? I like to think that as a friend, I would always help others in any way I could and go to the ends of the earth to support people but sadly what I was starting to realise is that sometimes others are not like that.

As my weight started to increase, I found myself with an internal battle going on. My husband had cheated so maybe it was because I was fat and pregnant? Maybe I needed to lose weight? But as I was missing my Mum and feeling insecure, I just ate more and put more weight on and then I would beat myself up.

It became like a vicious circle. I would try and look nice for when James came home from a flight, but everything would go unnoticed, so I would think what's the point? So, I would eat all the wrong food. Then I would start to feel worse and my self-esteem would start to fall again. It became a vicious circle.

But as each month progressed, I realised that I started to buy clothes that were baggy and bigger sizes because I just wanted to hide. I would buy lots of tracksuits and elasticated waists and dark colours. I thought doing this would help make me look fitter and slimmer. Of course, it never did and in fact, I just started to look like I couldn't be   bothered which was probably the truth.

My life was becoming literally all about the children. Even when James came home, I would still take the kids to preschool and the clubs and James would go to the gym and come along sometimes with me. Every now and again, I would think that maybe James was sorry and that there was hope still for our marriage but then we would have an argument about something and I would be left worrying and anxious.

I wasn't working at the time, other than just doing some podiatry on the side to bring in some extra money. We never seemed to have much money, but we seemed to manage, and the kids weren't wanting for anything. Grace was still in bed with me and this was my defence mechanism because although I certainly did not want my marriage to end, I just did not feel comfortable being in the same bed as my husband.

I felt like I still did not know the whole truth about his affair and every time I would still try and talk about it, I would get shouted at and told to move on and that he wanted to be with me.

I felt so low because I just felt like he had never acknowledged what he had done and almost just wanted to pretend that it had never happened but how could I ever forget? Gosh I missed my Mum! I desperately wanted someone that I could talk to and someone who would just hug me and tell me it would be ok.

My Mum was my soft place to fall and now I had no soft place. Don't get me wrong, I love my Dad and my sisters, but I don't think they understood what it was like to feel so betrayed. I was always someone who had put a smile on. I would wake up each morning, put my smile on and go out the front door! Stiff upper lip! Couldn't burden anyone with how I was feeling. I was a strong woman and could cope. But inside I was crumbling but I couldn't ever split my family up. Family was everything to me.

I remember one day when I dropped Harry off at preschool, he was being particularly anxious about me leaving him. He never seemed to cry but his anxiety levels always seemed high. Maybe he was picking up on the vibes at home? Grace wasn't even two and as I dropped Harry off on this day, my eyes filled with tears and the staff took me to one side. Grace was asleep in her pushchair, for a change, and the staff took me to a back room.

I just broke down. The floodgates opened, and I was shaking with tears. I could barely get my words out and had mascara running down my face. I told them that I was missing my Mum and then before I knew it, I was telling them all about James and how sad and lonely I felt. I just couldn't stop.

They brought in a box of tissues and I was rapidly going

through them. I think they were shocked as I was always so cheery and smiley because I hated to show any weakness, and I there I was crying my eyes out in their staff room. I felt angry at myself for showing them that I was weak and not the cheery, smiley person they thought.

However, they were lovely and allowed me the space to just let it out. They suggested marriage counselling and I thought maybe this was a good idea? Having someone who was not involved listen to me and maybe they could make James see what I needed. I just felt like there was no emotion at all and although he said he was sorry, I genuinely just felt these were words and that he wasn't really, and actually blamed me for making him have the affair due to being lonely and having no one to talk to at the time of the miscarriages. I dried my eyes and thanked the staff and went home with Grace.

When I got home, I looked up our local Relate and made an appointment. I was angry that I was the one who seemed to be making all the effort in saving our marriage as James was saying he wanted to but doing nothing about it. It is easy to say that you are sorry, and you will never do it again, but I sometimes wondered whether James just never ever wanted to talk about it again and just forget that it had ever happened.

I couldn't though because I was constantly questioning why it happened? I wanted James to show some emotion about it but there never seemed to be any other than if he got angry at me.

So, I made an appointment for the following week to go to marriage counselling with our local Relate. James went away on his trip to South Africa and again I was left at home with the kids wondering what he was up to?

I tried calling him late into the night and again there was no answer? Was I being paranoid now? Was he just asleep or was he out of the room? Was he in another room with someone else? I felt like I was losing control because the next day when I finally got hold of him, he told me he had been in his room again all the time.

The more I questioned him, the angrier he got at me for quizzing him. It always seemed to end in an argument about me asking him, not actually why I was asking him in the first place.

When James came back the following week, my Dad babysat for me and off we went to counselling. We sat in the waiting room in silence. I felt numb but also positive because surely this could really help us sort out our problems?

We entered a small room and sat beside each other with the counsellor in front of us. She was great in that she allowed both of us space to speak but what I found was that everything James was saying he felt, and was doing, was not corresponding to how he was acting at home. He showed me no emotion at home and I felt like I was merely existing with him, other than if we argued about my insecurity.

As the session progressed, I could feel myself getting more and more angry as I felt it was all show and lies. After the hour and it was time to leave, in the car on the way home, I turned to James and told him that if we went there again, I would leave him as I felt it was totally biased to him. I felt like James had put on this poor me facade and I felt so angry. I felt like the whole session was about him and why he had cheated and almost giving a reason why.

Now I am sure the counsellor would not have meant this to happen, but James seemed to act in such a way that appeared like the counsellor felt sorry for him. Looking back, I know this was not the case but James acting and looking like he was remorseful because to him, she was a position of authority and he didn't want her to think badly of him.

When we got home, I decided that I was literally going to exist for my children and do right by them because they deserved a family. Harry and Grace seemed very happy and that was all I cared about. I would get up each day, put my make up on and put my grey, baggy tracksuit on as wanted to be comfy! I used to be someone who really cared about their appearance, but I was now at the stage, where I would go a week and not wash my hair. I would just simply brush and put in a pony tail. I let the hair on my legs grow because let's face it, who else was going to see it?

Over the coming months, James' behaviour was becoming more distant and he was getting snappier. I felt like I was walking on egg shells and every time I would try and bring up anything, I would get sarcastic remarks or ignored. It was like a cycle after each trip. But I still wanted to be married.

I never really thought if I still loved James, it was more a case of being married so that's it, I just needed to get on with it. Time ticked on and Harry started school in the September. What a big milestone, and this meant that I now had a full day with Grace.

On one particular day, James was home from a trip and I had a podiatry appointment in someone's home to do their feet. James was to look after Grace and pick up Harry from school. At 3pm, I got this frantic phone call from James, saying he may be late picking Harry up and that I needed to pick him up. I asked why and what was wrong and was told in a firm voice, "I will tell you later".

I put the phone down and made my excuses and left to go and pick Harry up from school. When I got home, James was there with Grace. I ushered the kids to go and play in the lounge and asked what had happened. James had been caught leaving our local supermarket with a trolley full of food with

Grace sat in the trolley without paying for it. Security had pulled him back and questioned him and put Grace in another room. He told them he had forgotten to pay as Grace was crying and luckily, they had believed him. I was devastated with James.

What if they had pressed charges? We relied on his income to live and support our children. What kind of erratic behaviour was this? I felt stunned. The following week, we got a letter from the supermarket asking for a few hundred pound in charges for   security time lost in dealing with him.

I still have that letter today and still can't quite comprehend why he did that? In the following months, there seemed to be more and more strange behaviour and we were getting even more distant. Sometime James would hardly even speak to me and my focus as always was the children. He was becoming distant from them too.

One day, James was due back from Los Angeles. He usually sent me a short text, once he got in his car to drive home but on this day, I hadn't received anything. Initially, I just thought maybe his battery had died. As time progressed, I still hadn't heard anything. I tried calling his phone and went straight to voicemail. Again, I just thought maybe he had no battery and the traffic was bad on the way home. Three hours passed and still nothing. I was starting to worry as I thought what if he had had an accident?

So, I called the airline to see if there had been anything that had happened on the flight to delay the crew getting off. I spoke to their scheduling unit and was told all the crew had disembarked and nothing out of the ordinary on the flight.

I found myself questioning him again firmly saying "are you sure?" His reply in no uncertain terms was that the crew got off and his insinuation was that who knows where my husband is.

Another hour passed and by this stage, I could feel my anxiety growing. Where was he? This was not like him and very out of the ordinary. So, I called my local police station to explain that my husband should've been home but wasn't and I was worried as it was out of the ordinary to hear nothing.

They were lovely and very understanding. They asked for his car registration and the way he would travel home and then went off and contacted the paramedics to see if any crashes had been reported, as they said they record number plates.

When he came back on the line, he informed me that nothing had been reported. Another hour passed. It was now 5 hours since he should've been home. I contacted my Dad and I contacted my friends as I was getting so worried. I started to think I must try harder in my marriage and maybe things weren't so bad and that I should make more effort with how I look and make him feel special.

Then at 2pm, over six hours later than expected, my phone rang, and it was James. He was panting and sounded stressed, "I am on my way home", he said. "Where are you? Where have you been". I asked. What he told me next, I cannot even comprehend, even as I type because it was totally not what I expected. "I have killed someone" he shouted down the phone at me. "What?" I exclaimed! "I can't talk now because I am in shock, but a lady got off the aeroplane, tripped and then fell and banged her head, there was blood and then I had to perform CPR on her and I killed her". My head was spinning.

Was I hearing this right? My husband was telling me he had killed someone? "Are you ok to drive", I asked because I couldn't quite grasp the situation and was worried that maybe he was incapable of driving. "Yes, I am fine, I just want to get home". With that he hung up. I sat there in a daze. What had I just heard? I had so many emotions going through my head.

Now I had a medical background and I had worked for the airline myself for 9 years and this just did not make sense?

Killed someone? Performed CPR incorrectly? What? But why would my husband be lying? But it didn't make sense? But why would my husband lie? I felt so confused. On the one hand relief that he was ok and on his way home but killing someone? I had spoken to the airline and they had told me that there were no incidents?! Had they lied to me? Why would they lie though? They had nothing to gain from that?

Forty-five minutes later, James walked in the front door. He pushed passed me and took his shirt off and put it in the bin. "It's got blood on it" he informed me.

I looked him in the eye and asked him what had happened. "I don't want to talk about it", he replied. "I'm in shock". This didn't make sense, so I started to pursue it. "Please tell me what happened". James then proceeded to tell me about this old lady who he had been looking after all flight, tripped up on her way off the aeroplane and had banged her head.

Once she had banged her head and it was bleeding profusely, she started to arrest, and he had to perform CPR. I asked him where all the crew at this time there were as are 15 crew on board a jumbo jet, all of whom are first aid trained. He just replied that he didn't know. I asked how did he know that she was dead? "She just was" 'he shouted at me. "Who took her away then?" I asked, "Where were the paramedics?"

By this stage James was very agitated and started shouting at me, "I am in shock, stop questioning me. I have just had a three hour debrief from the airline and I don't want to talk about it anymore". With that he went upstairs to get changed leaving me stood at the bottom of the stairs bewildered and confused. None of it made sense.

The crew would have helped, the paramedics would have been there in minutes as was on the ground and they would have taken over. But why would my husband look me in the eye and lie about this? You did get a debrief when an emergency happened but then why had the airline told me there were no emergencies? My head hurt with questions and confusion.

My gut was telling me this was all lies but surely no one would lie about this? Who would go to such extreme lengths like this? Surely if you were late, you would just say there was a traffic jam and my battery died? Maybe it was true? Maybe it was that far out, that it was true? But it just didn't make sense logically?

That night James barely spoke to me. I kept asking if he was alright and he would just mumble about being in shock as he had killed this lovely old lady. The next morning, I just did not want to let this go as it seemed so surreal. I asked James to call his airline because I said that it was wrong that in such emergencies, when the crew were to be this delayed, that they did not inform next of kin.

I told him I had called the airline and that they had told me that there were no incidents. He got snappy at me and just said he didn't know why they said that because there was this medical emergency. As he was saying all of this, the words of the man in the scheduling unit ran in my ears, "there are no emergencies or any delays from the Los Angeles flight, all crew disembarked as normal". Who was lying? Him? My husband? But why would my husband lie to such extreme?

I was so confused. James refused to call the airline and I said they should call him then on his days off to check on him. Having flown myself previously, I knew their procedures were that if there was an emergency, they would contact the crew on their days off to check they were ok. During James three days off, we did not get any calls from the airline. The more I pushed James, the angrier he got at me. It got so bad, I daren't mention it again.

On the day of his next trip, I said that he needed to see his line manager to say that they should've informed the next of kin. I was still feeling so confused as my gut was still saying this wasn't true, but James was still looking me in the eye swearing blind it did.

When James got to work, I got a phone call about two hours after he left. "You will never believe this" he said. "What?" I asked. "The lady who I performed CPR on, she is actually alive and in hospital and is so grateful to me for saving her life". Had I heard that right? From killing her a few days previously to now being a hero as he had saved her life? I asked him "How did she get taken away when you left after you did CPR? Was she on a gurney with a blanket over her?". James started to get agitated and annoyed at me again. "Look she's alive and that's all there is to it".

With that he hung up and went on his flight. I didn't know whether to laugh or cry? What was my life coming to? My husband swore blind this happened! Why would he lie about that? He had lied before and his behaviour was very erratic but surely there are easier lies? I felt so confused.

I told my best friend and my Dad and we both questioned whether it was real but again, why would he lie to that degree? I couldn't keep questioning him, so I just had to put it in a box and get on with being the best Mum I could to Grace and Harry. I needed to just get on with it. I wanted to keep my family together. I needed to forget about it for my own sake because what would the alternative be

Chapter 4 - My Worst Nightmare Was Coming True

As the days progressed, I was literally losing myself before my eyes. I was gaining weight and I wasn't bothered. I hated the way I looked. Why would James treat me like he had if I was attractive? Maybe it was my fault I was now in a loveless marriage? I pretty much wore baggy   grey tracksuits each day with my hair in a ponytail. What was the point of making an effort?

It was comfy clothes to be Mum to Harry and Grace. I hated looking at myself in the mirror because I didn't even recognise myself. I had always been so interested in fashion and make up and always prided myself on trying to look good, but I was not bothered anymore. James was away so much, and things were deteriorating between us. Every time I tried to talk, I was shut down.

It was like he had no emotion around our marriage. I even tried to buy some sexy underwear to see if I could maybe try and rekindle what I thought we had when we first met, but all of this was to no avail. He was just not interested. So, I continued to do what I felt safe about and that was being a Mum.

One day James informed me he was leaving a day early to go to work. I asked him why and where he was staying? He replied that a friend of his called Gavin had given him his flat key in London as he lived in France and said that he could stay there.

James told me that he had just flown with Gavin and explained to him the problems we were having, and Gavin had kindly offered him to stay at his flat if he needed space.

Now I had flown with Gavin many years previously when I worked for the airline and always remembered him being a nice guy and could imagine him being nice like that. James said it was a positive thing as it would give us both space and time to think.

I did wonder that as he was away so much anyway, why would he want any more space, but I didn't dare say that to him. So off James went a day earlier leaving me to explain to the kids as to why Daddy had gone already.

This started to become a pattern more and more before James trip and sometimes he would even go there directly after a flight. I said to James, "Are you sure that Gavin doesn't mind you staying? Are you giving him any money?". James response was that Gavin just wanted what was best for us both and he was happy to help us in any way he could. I felt so empty inside.

Although the trust from James affair had been broken, I still wanted to be married. It all just seemed so wrong and not how I ever envisaged my marriage to be. How had it come to this? What had I done wrong? Could I have been a better wife? I was missing my Mum so much. She would know what to do.

Other than my children, I was getting no physical contact from anyone with cuddles and I felt so desperately lonely.

This was not how I envisaged my life when I was growing up.

Days passed by and turned into weeks. I had been given the name of a local counsellor who had been a practising psychotherapist but was now retired and was giving free counselling sessions at our local church. I thought this had to be worth a try again and mentioned it to James who seemed a little taken aback, but he did say he was willing to go.

So, we started having some sessions together. They were only an hour, but these ones seemed to delve a bit deeper. We even started to have some separately as well, as the counsellor advised that may help. I found these useful as it was finally like I could off load to someone who had no emotional involvement.

As the months progressed, James' time in our home was becoming less frequent but just enough that I kept thinking maybe things would be OK in the end, and that maybe it was a good thing he was spending so much time thinking as he may realise what he wants and what he has?

The kids didn't seem to bother that Daddy was away even more as I suppose this was just how it was, and nothing really had changed as they had no concept of time. Every time James left for work, I thought would this be the time he would have an epiphany and next time he came home, he would be all apologetic and tell me he loved me and that he was sorry and wanted to be with me and call me beautiful. That moment just never came.

One day I got a letter from our bank about our overdraft and money had always worried me and I needed to speak to James. He was in Hong Kong and as I looked at my watch, I realised it was midnight there. Now I knew James didn't need much sleep and thought about time differences and thought maybe he would be up anyway with jet lag?

So, I called the hotel and asked to be put through to James' room. The phone rang and rang and rang and went through to his rooms voicemail. Where was he? It was midnight? Maybe he was out partying with the crew as I know this could happen sometimes but still, it was midnight?

My heart started to pound. All the trust issues came flooding back. Was he with someone? Was he fast asleep? But no, he would hear the phone as I knew this hotel and the rooms were small. I felt so confused. Was I going crazy?! Was I overreacting?

I tried to go back to Grace and Harry and play with them and thought I will leave it a few hours and try calling again.

At what would be 2am Hong Kong time, I tried again. No answer. Where was he? I was starting to feel sick. Was I stupid? Was I naive to the fact that my husband could be with another woman? I tried to push all these thoughts out of my mind. I started to get tea ready for Harry and Grace and thought again, I will call in a few hours. Surely then he would answer? So, I made tea with my heart pounding, a sick feeling in my stomach whilst trying to be fun and happy Mummy to my children.

None of this was their fault and I needed to be the best Mum I could to them. After tea, I tried calling the hotel again. No answer. By now, I didn't know whether to be worried? I couldn't call hotel security could I to ask them to check on him? What if he was dead? No, I couldn't ask the hotel to do that, they would think I was crazy! Maybe I was?

Hours passed and every few hours I tried calling his room and would get no answer. Then on the sixth occasion which was 11am Hong Kong time and now middle of the night for me, James picked up the phone. "Where have you been I asked?". James replied in a shocked voice "In my room". Had I heard that right? He had been in his room all the time? I questioned him and told him I had been trying to call for the last 10 hours!

James told me that when he woke up, the phone receiver must have got knocked off his hotel phone as it was on the floor. I questioned James and asked why the phone rang several times and went to voicemail rather than an engaged tone or straight to voicemail?

James started to get angry at me and said, "I have been here sleeping all the time!" Why was my gut saying this wasn't true? Why would my husband lie though? So, I thought I would try and bluff him, so I told him I had called hotel security, they had gone to knock on his room door and then when there was no answer, they went in and he wasn't there.

James really started to get angry then, "Are you calling me a liar" he shouted. Why would he react like this if he wasn't there? "I am telling you I have been in this room the whole time!" Maybe he was telling the truth, after all I hadn't had hotel security and maybe he had knocked the phone over?

"OK" I quietly replied. James calmed down and we had a conversation about the bank and then we said our goodbye and I put the phone down. I felt numb! I couldn't even cry as I felt that numb. What was wrong with me? Caroline you are not crazy! Why was I always thinking the worst! James was trying and there I was questioning him again! With that I lay down and with sheer exhaustion, I fell asleep.

When James arrived home, we never even mentioned the "phone" incident at all. It was just brushed away like it had never happened. But it had happened. It had made me question my sanity again. It had made me question my husband again. It had made me question my marriage again.

Was this now my life? Living on eggshells? Not daring to ask anything because I would get shouted out and told I was crazy! But my gut was telling me something was not right. I felt so anxious, but I did not want my family to split up, so I shelved it all in a little box and focused on my children.

Summer was coming up and Will was now 6. Grace had just turned 3. I adored my children and they brought me so much joy. I felt like I was made to be a Mum and I had the best relationship with my kids.

Everyday though as I was watching them grow up, I was tinged with an ache in my heart that my Mum was not there to see them blossom. Grace was like a mini me and my Mum would have loved seeing the similarities and equally as she had never had a son, the joy of watching Harry grow up.

James would often get jealous of this and tell me that the kids loved me more. I tried to explain that I was their Mum and always at home but that because of his job, it was harder, but they still loved him equally so. I almost felt like James was angry at me that the kids always asked for their Mum if they hurt themselves.

As a family, we loved camping and we had a mid-week break booked at a campsite in Oxford that we had been to before and the kids and I were excited about going. We were on countdown and couldn't wait. James arrived back from his trip on the Friday and we were to leave the afternoon of the next day.

I had got all the food in and pretty much all packed up, all we needed to do was load the trailer and off we could go. Maybe this would be a good chance to try and reconnect with James?

He had been so distant recently that I felt we were drifting even further apart. He was still sleeping in the spare bedroom as Grace was still in bed with me. Maybe she was my security blanket and my reason not to share a bed with him?

As I tucked Harry and Grace in that night, we chatted about all the exciting things we would do whilst we were away. James was downstairs and seemed disinterested in the impending holiday, but I kept the excitement going for the kid's sake. I loved seeing their excited faces and they both seemed so happy. I kissed them goodnight and went downstairs.

The atmosphere was really strange. I tried to talk to James, but he was dismissive and didn't seem interested, so I just went up to bed to watch tv and said I would see him in the morning. I struggled to sleep nowadays and had to be at the point of exhaustion to fall asleep and so I would watch television until late in the night, when I could then barely keep my eyes open and then literally turn the TV off and fall asleep.

When I woke in the morning, Grace was smiling at me and as Harry had heard we were awake, he came running in all excited! Both children were early risers and it was still 6.30am but nothing was going to dampen our excitement! I started to sing Cliff Richard's "We're all going on a summer holiday".

The kids were jumping up and down on the bed and it was just such a joy to see. Harry said he was going to wake his Daddy and off he went. "Where's Dad?" I heard Harry shout. I got out of bed and went to the spare bedroom. The bed was empty. Where was James? I went downstairs to see if there was a note. Nothing.

My heart started pounding and my breathing was getting heavy. Where the hell was he? I was a mixture of angry and anxious. Harry looked at me and asked, "Are we still going on holiday?". "Of course," I answered. What else could I say? I tried to call James' mobile and it went straight through to voicemail, I left an angry message this time. What was he doing!? How dare he do this on the day of our holiday? Where was he? I wondered maybe if he had gone to a local hotel as we had two literally next to where we lived.

I quickly got dressed and put the kids in the car and drove to them to see if I could see his car. The kids were getting upset and asking where Daddy was, and I kept saying I don't know. I refused to lie to them. I kept reassuring them that no matter what, we would absolutely be going on holiday that day.

We went back home, and I kept calling his number, no answer! I called my sister at 10am in tears and said to her what had happened. I said to her that I didn't think I could keep doing this, but I just couldn't survive financially on my own. I felt so stuck and lonely and like I was in this long dark tunnel with the only light being my children. I felt better having talked to her, but I was feeling sick. How could he do this to us?

This time he had really upset the children. I felt so protective over them and they did not deserve this. As I sat thinking about his behaviour, I realised that it was getting worse. He had been really snappy with the kids for the last six months as well and was leaving early for his flights and arriving back later. I was still so surprised that Gavin would just let him have a key and allow him to stay for free?

As the hours passed, I started to actual think that what if he didn't come home? How was I going to put the tent up on my own? I refused to let my kids down, so no matter what, we were going on holiday. I called my friends who were also avid campers as I knew they were going to another campsite and asked if I rebooked to their campsite, would they be able to help me with the tent.

They were lovely and said absolutely, so now I knew I had options. We would be sleeping in a tent that night if it killed me!

Then at 11.30am my phone rang, and it was James. This time I let rip. He had hurt the children. "Where the hell have you been" I shouted down the phone. "I went to Gavin's" he replied. I lost it with him and said how dare he do that to us on the night before we were going on holiday and told him how upset the kids were. It all seemed to fall on deaf ears as he remained really calm, told me he was on his way home and he was still coming with us on holiday and hung up.

I called my friend and my sister to say, holiday was back on and he was on his way home. I spoke to my Dad and always tried to shield him from a lot as just didn't want to worry him as I know he was really struggling to cope with the loss of my Mum and I didn't want to burden him.

When James arrived home, I said we needed to talk. I settled the kids in front of the television and we went and sat in the kitchen. I questioned again where he had been. James told me that he couldn't get to sleep the night before and that he needed some space between us, so he could think. My heart was pounding.

He told me he loved me and that he was sorry and that we were to have a great holiday. I told him "You can't keep doing this to me and especially not now you are involving the children". James nodded and told me he definitely wanted to be with me and that he loved me and wanted our marriage to work. Maybe this was going to be the start of a new chapter for us?

So, we got all our stuff together, loaded up the trailer and off we went to Oxford. We were there until the Friday and we had lots of activities planned to do. The campsite was so child friendly with an amazing park for the kids and they loved it. James seemed distant and kept wandering off. It was like it was Harry, Grace and me and then James in a world of his own.

Every morning, he would wake up and tell us he was going to get a newspaper and be gone for ages! I tried not to think about it because my focus was on the kids having a fun time, which they were in abundance.

One of the days, we went to a local farm and went strawberry picking. Again, it was Harry, Grace and I all chatting together picking and eating the strawberries and James would be about 10 metres away on his own. The kids didn't seem to notice but I did. I felt like I was walking on eggshells as just didn't know what was going on.

On the final day, we packed up all our camping stuff, loaded the car and trailer up and drove home. When we got home, I said to James "What is going on, do you not want to be with me?" James looked me right in the eye and said "Of course I do, I love you and I love our family. It's just going to take time for us to get back to how we were." I wasn't convinced because I was starting to think I couldn't ever remember a time when we were happy but again, I didn't want to break my daily life up and I am certainly not a quitter. My kids need both parents in their life however, that was to be.

The next day we all woke up and seemed an eerie calm in the house. I had a podiatry appointment with someone locally so at 10.30am, I left and said I would be back in an hour and a half. When I came back home, Grace was having a nap and Harry was watching the television in the lounge. James was sat in the kitchen.

As I came in, James got up and stood against the kitchen counter. "I need to talk" he said. My heart started pounding and I felt sick. "I'm leaving" he said looking at me in the eye. For a split second, I thought this can't be happening, and my family can't split up, but I found myself replying, "Yes you are". We both sat down at the kitchen table and it felt so weird.

I said to him that I would never stop him seeing the children as I really felt the importance of both parents being in a child's life. He got up and said, "tell the kids I am going to work early." This had been the usual request from James in the last 6 months and I would dutifully just tell the kids that he had gone early. "Not this time" I replied. "You need to tell the children".

Grace was till sleeping, but James shouted to the lounge and called Harry in. I will never forget the next moment as James informed Harry that he was leaving for good. Harry dropped to his knees and shouted NO! Harry started to cry, and I got up to cuddle him.

With that James went upstairs, packed a bag and he left within ten minutes of telling us all.

I cuddled Harry and told him it would all be ok. That Mummy and Daddy still loved him and Grace more than anything and it was not his fault. That sometimes adults change but it does not change them as a Mum or Dad and a different kind of love. He seemed to perk up as ultimately, James not being around was normal to him anyway. Off he trotted into the lounge and just started watching television.

I felt numb. My marriage had ended. There was no going back now. I sat there staring into space for what seemed like an eternity. Grace started to wake up and I went upstairs to get her. I scooped her up and held her tight. My children were so innocent, and they now had a single Mum to take care of them. I went downstairs and called my Dad and my friend. I truly didn't know what to do with myself. My friend came over and sat with me until my Dad came.

I was trying not to cry because the reality of what was happening seemed so unreal. I was now a single parent!

My kids were going to grow up in a broken home. All my worst nightmares were coming true. When I was growing up playing with my dolls, I imagined getting married to Prince Charming and living happily ever after and now all of that was shattered. I had such a negative view of single Mums, for whatever reason, I don't even know why, but now I was one! Thank goodness my Mum was not alive to see this.

When my Dad arrived, we sat at the kitchen table to make some contingency plans. I was so scared about the finances more than anything. However, it was Saturday so there was no one really I could call to speak to, so I had a pen and a pad and made a list for Monday.

I knew I could now get tax credits but how much? I could get a reduction on my council tax, but how much? So many unanswered questions and just all seemed so overwhelming. Harry and Grace seemed absolutely fine.

They were playing and watching television whilst I was in the kitchen with my Dad. I now had my list and my Dad said to me, "are you sure you can't work this out?" I could tell he felt ashamed as my marriage had broken down. He was old school that once you were married, you were married for life and didn't understand all this divorce aspect.

I felt such a failure. Why me? What had I done wrong for our marriage to fail? Could I have done more to save it? The only saving Grace, I had in my head was that I didn't quit. He was the one who walked away not me. I was prepared to stay unhappy and lonely because I thought this was the best for the children.

I made the kids their tea and I wasn't hungry. My tummy was

in knots. My hands were shaky and sweaty, and I just didn't know what the future would hold. I wanted to stay in the house. I don't think I could've coped if we had to move. It was hard enough processing the fact that I was now a single Mum.

As bedtime drew close for the children, Harry was upstairs brushing his teeth, when I heard him shouting "Mummy, Mummy, come quick". I dashed upstairs wondering what had happened? Had he hurt himself? He was in my bedroom down the side of my bed shouting, "Come and look?"

As I walked around I saw a pool of blood on the carpet and next to the blood was one of our cats and 6 kittens! The cat had given birth! I didn't know whether to laugh or cry!?

This was the last thing I needed but Harry and Grace were delighted and in the darkest of days, my children were smiling and excited about the kittens. I took the cat and the kittens downstairs and googled what I should do! I didn't have a clue.

I didn't even know the cat was pregnant! I got a cardboard box, put a blanket in it and put Fluffy and her kittens in the box. The children were in their element, naming them and getting excited. I didn't have the heart to tell them, that no way were we keeping any but that was for another day.

I tucked Grace and Harry in bed and crawled into my bed and the tears started. I don't know how long I lay there crying but it seemed like an eternity. How had my life turned out like this?

Why was this happening to me? I was a nice person! I treated people nicely! I just sobbed until I had no tears left and I must've fallen asleep from sheer exhaustion.

The next day was Sunday and again, I couldn't do anything,

but I had been invited to a party at our local community centre with the kids, and my friends were going and they persuaded me to still go.

I felt so numb. It was like I was having an out of body experience. I was going through the motions but it just all felt so surreal. I could tell everyone was staring at me. Looking at me in a way of pity.

Poor Caroline. Poor single Mum, wrecked marriage Caroline. It was like I was the topic of conversation. I felt fat, I felt alone, I felt scared and I felt so anxious. What exactly did the future now hold for me and how the hell was I going to survive financially?

Chapter 5 -Depths of Darkness

Monday morning came, and I got snacks for the kids, got them settled with loads of activities in the lounge and I got my iPad and went and sat down at the kitchen table. I had woken that morning with pins and needles in my hands and thought I must have slept funny.

My breathing was really shallow, but I just thought it was nerves and all this uncertainty about our future. I had heard nothing at all from James since he had left. This was real. We were definitely split up. One good thing was that I thought that he was the one that left. This now gave me the green light to get a divorce because I wasn't the quitter.

I wasn't the one that had broken our family up and for some reason at this time, this was so important to me. I may have been desperately sad and lonely, but we don't quit in our family and at least I could say that to my Dad.

I got the telephone and sat staring at it. It was all so overwhelming. I felt like I had no energy, but this family relied upon me now. there was no one else. If I didn't do it, then it wasn't going to get done. I had a big list of people to call. I needed to know where I stood legally and financially. One of my friends had given me the number of a divorce lawyer she had used, and she did a free consultation, so that was my first phone call.

She was lovely and reassured me about the main issues like I could stay in the house if I wanted. I was really fixated on the house because I wanted as least disruption for Harry and Grace as possible. I needed to shield them as much as I could because they didn't deserve a life from a broken family, and I wanted to do everything in my power to make sure they knew how much I loved them and would never let them down.

The whole day was spent on the phone, calling utilities, council tax, banks, everyone I could think of. The first time I told someone on the phone that my husband had just left, I thought they would start judging me and think I was one of those single Mums. I had this real issue about being a single Mum!

But everyone was so nice. In fact, they were all so lovely that they made me feel a bit better as they were telling me how sorry they were, and they were all so helpful. From those phone calls, I managed to shave off over £200 on my bills. Result! However, as I was working out all the debt we had, my head fell in my hands!

The total amount of debt was £73,000. How could I afford any of that? I only worked very part time and that was when James was at home. How was I going to cope? The thought of childcare scared me so much as my children had never been in childcare because I was always around. How was I going to cope paying the bills, paying the mortgage and putting food on the table? I contacted all the creditors and found that £23,000 was in my sole name and what I was liable for.

James was liable for all the rest. I felt sick. It felt like the world was crashing down around me. This was our home. This was where Harry and Grace felt settled but what was I going to do? My heart was pounding, and my hand felt so tingly. I started to clench my fists to try and get the circulation going again. I was trying desperately not to cry in front of Harry and Grace as this was not their problem.

They didn't ask to be in a broken home. I needed to ensure that they knew they were loved to the moon and back and I never wanted them to feel anything less than the special children they were. God, I missed my Mum. Just to feel her arms around me and not even to give me advice but to just hold me. Her arms were my safe place, but I no longer felt safe anywhere.

I started to work out a budget. It didn't look good. My outgoings were way more than my income. I had to stay in the house though. I needed to do more podiatry, but I needed to pick my kids up from school? How was I going to cope? It all seemed so complicated and overwhelming! I felt like I had permanent butterflies in my stomach and I just couldn't eat.

I contacted tax credits and they filed in all the forms for me and said it would be 6 weeks processing before first payment. I ended that day feeling so low. I had never imagined that I would ever be having these conversations with people about money and bills and tax credits.

I had never had any benefits all my life! I looked up at the sky and said to my Mum, "You were right about making me do podiatry as my degree". My Mum had always wanted me and my two sisters to get degrees because she hadn't had that opportunity as she had to leave school at 16 and help her Mum, my grandma as she was a single Mum.

She always said we all had to get a degree because that way we were all independent and need never have to rely on anyone because we could look after ourselves. She was sort of right. I was lucky in that I had a profession but even with what I could earn?, the bills and mortgage seemed so huge.

Grace had always been in bed with me and I don't know why but I decided to choose this time to put her in her own bed in her own bedroom. I needed some space in my bedroom. I needed somewhere I could cry and cry some more.

I wondered how she would be as she had slept beside me for so long and I couldn't believe it that she went straight in and went to sleep! I was ready for a back and forth but at least that was less stressful for me.

I went to bed that night with what felt like the worries of the world on my shoulders! I put the telly on and sat watching it. I don't even remember what was on but I daren't lie down to sleep unless I was literally closing my eyes because I knew that my mind would be going ten to the dozen and I would just get more upset. Again, I must've fallen asleep due to sheer exhaustion.

When I woke up the next morning, it was even earlier than usual. I felt weird. My heart was racing, my hands were tingling, and my breathing was so shallow. I got up and went into my ensuite. "Breathe" I said to myself. But I was struggling to catch my breath.

What was happening? My breathing started to get faster and faster as I was trying to catch my breath. It felt like my head was going to explode and my heart seemed like it was beating so loudly in my head. I sat on the floor next to the toilet and cupped my hands together. I started to try and breathe into my hands. I was getting scared.

I had Grace and Harry to look after, I needed to get a grip. It seemed like an eternity but was probably only for a few minutes that I was breathing into my hands and my breathing started to slow down. What was that? Had I just had a panic attack? I had never had one before, but I knew about them from my medical background. I sat there with tears streaming down my face. Was this my life? I felt so out of control.

Money, marriage, job, I felt like I was drowning. What exactly in my life was I in control of? I felt myself start to panic again and with that I started scratching hard on my thighs.

Harder and harder and my legs were getting red and starting to hurt but it was numbing everything else out because in that moment, all I was focused on was making my thighs bleed.

Faster and faster I started to scratch until I looked down and my thighs were bleeding. I had never done that before but in that moment, I felt a lightness. That all the emotional pain had gone away and I was just thinking about the physical pain I had on my thighs. I looked at my legs and started crying.

What was I doing? I felt so desperately alone and lost. I slowly got up and got dressed. The kids were still asleep. I stood in front of the mirror and put some make up on. I looked purely at the make-up that I was putting on, the mask to hide my sadness but I couldn't truly look at myself because I felt disgusted. I thought I looked disgusting. Ugly and fat and horrible. I didn't want to look at myself.

As I finished getting ready, Grace and Harry woke up and I gave them both a big cuddle. They had no clue what had just happened on my bathroom floor and I certainly did not want them seeing their Mum like that. I was their rock, their security blanket.

Days passed and what I thought was maybe a one off start to my day, started to be the norm for me. I would wake up in the morning with my heart pounding, my hands filled with pins and needles struggling to catch my breath. I would go in sit in the exact same place each morning and most mornings I would have a panic attack. Some were longer than others and some days, I just managed to catch them before I lost control of my breathing.

When the panic attack was bad, this was when I felt the most out of control and where I would literally scratch my legs until they bled. It was like a surge of calm that would come over me.

The only thing was because I was so anxious, I was biting my nails so much that on one morning, I was really struggling to make my thighs bleed. I needed to make them bleed! This was the only way to calm me down after a panic attack so I grabbed the toothpaste and with the sharp corners of the toothpaste, I plunged it back and forth on my leg.

These cuts were deeper and funnily enough less blood, but the pain was searing and again for a few moments, all I could think about was the pain in my legs.

I would get up, put my make up with the least amount of eye contact with myself in the mirror and then get dressed. Dressed into my tracksuits. Why would anyone look at me? I was a single Mum so why bother even trying?

Work wise, I managed to get a clinical day on a Friday at a clinic, but this meant I needed childcare. Now I was looking after my friends two children a lot and as I told her my worries, she said she would have them and I said I would pay.

Now she never paid me for having her children, but I thought I should pay her for some reason. She readily agreed so when I was in my clinic each Friday, Natalie would pick up Grace and Harry and take them home for tea. I was really struggling with money and as I was self-employed, I dreaded any of the kids being poorly as I couldn't work then which meant I wouldn't get paid.

James rang infrequently, and I kept asking him when he was going to come and see the children and I kept getting vague answers. He told me he was still staying at Gavin's place.

The children seemed fine although they did ask occasionally when they would see their father and I kept saying he was away on a trip which strictly speaking he was. Then one day, James told me he was coming up to see the children.

In my wisdom at the time, I said he could come in the house and I would go around to my Dad's, so he could have some quality time with the children. This is exactly what happened. I thought I was doing the right thing but in hindsight, I think this was more confusing for them seeing Daddy at home. This carried on for a few months and things were not awful between James and me, but very tense.

I was feeling very numb and raw and James seemed to just want me to get on with it as he never asked about anything. I checked with child maintenance how much he should pay me, and he started to pay me what he legally had to.

One day I was at my friend's house with Grace and Harry and James was coming up to see them at 5pm for tea in the house. It was about midday and suddenly I got a text through on my phone from James. "Hi sexy lady, how are you? I'm missing you so much". My heart stopped, and I re-read it and double checked who it was from.

I showed my friend. I honestly didn't know whether to laugh or cry! I knew it! Was I really that stupid thinking he had been staying at Gavin's? This text was clearly not for me! I said to my friend, "I'm not going to reply. I'm going to see if he admits it!" It was like a big weight had been lifted because I genuinely thought that when he left and was saying he needed space and time on his own, that just didn't ring true.

James had never seemed to have any gaps where he had been on his own and my suspicions were right all along. It was like a vindication for me. I wasn't going crazy! My gut was right! But did this mean that my gut was right on all the other occasions as well?

We sat there, whilst our children played waiting for James to realise that he had sent me the wrong text and sure enough a few hours later, I got another text. This time, it was clearly meant for me. "I know you know. Meet me at the house at 5pm and leave the kids at your friends".

I just responded with an "Ok". What was I to do? I felt so numb and so low that I just wanted to curl up and shut the world out. But I couldn't because I had Grace and Harry relying upon me. So at 4.30pm, I went alone back home. I went up to James bedroom and got three bin bags and filled them all with his clothes and any other things I thought he may want.

I dragged them downstairs and had them all in the hallway. James arrived at 5pm and knocked on the door even though he had a key. Things had now changed. I opened the door and in walked James. He stood on one side of the hall and I stood on the other. I asked him for his phone as it was in my name and his front door key. He must've known I was going to ask, as he had them both ready. I said to him, "How could he?".

He just looked at me so coldly that it gave me shivers. He shrugged his shoulders. He had his arms folded and was standing leaning against the wall. I told him I would be starting divorce proceedings on the ground of adultery and again he just shrugged. He told me he wasn't going to see the kids that day and that he had met someone and was living with them. I asked if he had ever stayed with Gavin and was that all lies, and he just smirked at me.

I couldn't believe the man I had married and had children with was stood in front of me treating me like this. I said to him "I don't even want to imagine how many affairs you have had in my marriage?" He looked me in the eye, with his arms folded and said to me, "Well, that is none of your business".

Wow! Had I heard, that right? What was real in my marriage? With that James gathered all the bin bags up and walked out and slammed the door leaving me stunned!

Why was he treating me like this? I wasn't the one that had lied and cheated? What gave him the right to speak to me like that? Had he no respect? I was the mother of his children. I was in shock.

Part of me was so pleased that I finally knew the truth and then the other half was "What exactly was my marriage?". We had been married for 12 years! I tried to think when it had gone wrong and I just couldn't pin point it. It seemed like as long as I could remember. We hadn't had a marriage for years.

This wasn't what marriage was all about. I felt so numb, but I needed to go and collect Grace and Harry. I went around to my friends and told her what had happened, and she was shocked. How could he do this to me and the children?! I took Grace and Harry home and cooked tea and put them to bed.

My daily diet at this stage was now wine, sweet chilli Snack-a-Jacks and cheese and chive dip. I would get a tray, go upstairs, get ready for bed and put the telly on. I don't think I even remember what I was watching but it was better than the alternative of thinking about my train track life. I was really struggling for money and even when I went to put petrol in the car, I only ever dared put £10 in because I wondered if I would need the money the next day.

For the next few months, each morning I would wake up early

with pins and needles and feeling out of breath and get in my usual position on my bathroom floor and have a panic attack and make my legs bleed. It was almost becoming a habit and the one thing in my life that was mine and that I had total control over.

I felt ashamed of what was happening to me and what I was doing as I thought everyone would think I was weak for not coping. I went back to see my counsellor and I told him that I was really struggling. Why was James not showing any signs of remorse? Why would he not acknowledge what he had done? I almost felt by the way he was behaving that everything was my fault.

My counsellor took me by the shoulders and told me he thought James had a personality disorder and to go and google narcissism when I got home. He told me that James would never feel remorse or apologise as he was not capable and that I should stop wasting my time expecting him to.

When I got home, I googled what the counsellor had told me, and it was like reading about James! Everything I read, I thought this is my marriage and the scary part was that they all said get away from them but if you had children, this was going to be the challenge.

It was a relief that it wasn't me being crazy but equally scary as I read what the future could hold. I started crying. It scared me that James would never show regret or remorse, yet I had to stay in contact because I needed to discuss the children with him. Maybe it wouldn't be as bad as the all the literature said? Maybe it would be all nice and amicable once the dust settled?

My counsellor told me I needed to see someone on a more professional basis as he could see I was struggling. So, I booked in to see a psychotherapist. I knew I needed some help, but I had to keep going for my children.

When I saw her, she was so nice and friendly. The first session she asked me a whole list of questions to see how depressed I was. When she looked though the answers, she looked up and said, "If you didn't have children, Caroline, I would be taking you directly to the hospital right now." I asked her what she meant, and she told me I was clinically depressed. I was running on empty.

We started to talk about my last few years with my Mum and then everything that had happened with James. The erratic behaviour, the lies, the cheating and being angry at me for even daring to question him.

She looked at me and said, "You do know you have been the victim of emotional abuse and have been bullied?" I looked at her in shock, "No, you must have it wrong I said, it was just disagreements and me questioning him about what he was doing." She looked me in the eye and said' "Caroline, this is exactly what manipulation is all about.

Slowly chipping away at your confidence with lies, arguments and erratic behaviour leaving you questioning what is real and what is not. You are not crazy, Caroline. You were emotionally abused." I sat there motionless, I was in shock. I thought back to the woman I was before we got married.

Confident, ambitious and with a real zest for life. I started crying. What had happened to me? How could I not see this? Why had I allowed this to happen? I started to get angry, not at James but at myself. I was an intelligent woman so how had I allowed that to happen?

The psychotherapist told me that I had PTSD, post-traumatic stress disorder. Everything was all starting to piece together. I left the session feeling numb. I had PTSD, I had clinical depression, I had been emotionally abused. It was like I was having an out of body experience. This was not how my life was meant to turn out. I didn't know whether to feel better that there was a reason I was feeling how I was. But I just kept thinking I was a strong, independent woman so how the hell was I now so broken and at rock bottom?

The next few months were so hard because I started divorce proceedings with the help of my Dad and James started to see Grace and Harry but this time he would knock at the door and take them out. We didn't really speak at the door, but he would text, and it would almost be like he wanted an argument.

It seemed whatever I said was wrong and as much as I would try to be amicable, even though I felt angry at him, it was like he just wanted to keep fighting and having long text battles and I kept feeling like I was having to defend myself. I really thought he would be fine with communicating about the children, but there always seemed to be an issue or problem and it always seemed to be my fault.

I felt drained and exhausted and every time my phone went, and I could see it was from James, my heart would start racing and my breathing would get quicker.

James started to ask if he could take Harry and Grace down as he wanted to introduce them to his girlfriend, Tracey. My heart sank, I knew this day would come but still they were my babies! I said yes but I would need an address as they lived two hours away.

James told me that Tracey was not ready to give me her address. "What does she think I am going to do? I just want to know where my children will be that's all." I replied. James refused to give it to me, so I refused to let Harry and Grace go.

This carried on for six weeks until one day, when James was seeing them after school, when he dropped them off home, he thrust a piece of paper into my hand with Tracey's address on it. This time I had to say yes, and we arranged the following weekend for Harry and Grace to go down to stay with them over night.

My heart was breaking. My children were going to be playing happy families with someone else. Someone that my husband had cheated for months with and I just had to accept it. How would I cope? My kids were with me all the time bar school and I was used to being there for them.

This was a huge step for me, but I knew I had to overcome. I had always said, that it is so important for Grace and Harry to keep contact with their Dad and whilst I felt I had been the one to keep pushing James to see them for the first six months, I tried to see the positive in that they were going there for the weekend.

The weekend arrived and that morning, I had the biggest panic attack. I was dying inside but trying to be all excited for Grace and Harry. They seemed very apprehensive and kept saying they didn't want to go but I tried to reassure them, and James was picking them up at 10am. We were all ready way too early as I had bags packed with their teddy and moomoo in as I wanted them to have as many home comforts there as they could.

I had never even met or spoken to Tracey and part of me was glad I never did and the other part was thinking, I am trusting you with the most precious people in my life. I felt sick. Grace was playing in the kitchen and the sun was beating in. Grace asked me, "Mummy, what's Fluffy doing in the garden?" Both of our cats were outside and Stig was wandering around and Fluffy was lying in the corner in the sun. But as I looked out of the window, it didn't look like Fluffy was moving?!

Grace started to open the patio doors to go outside and I

stopped her. "You stay here Grace and make sure your brother is ready." I stepped outside and started to walk towards Fluffy. I looked down and her eyes were open and there was no movement. I got a stick and poked her. She was as stiff as a board. She was dead. I didn't know whether to laugh or cry?!

My kids were spending the night away from me for the very first time ever in their life and I had a dead cat in my garden. I looked up at the sky and in my head, I was saying "why me"? I couldn't believe that of all days for this to happen it was today.

I went back into the kitchen where Grace asked about Fluffy. "She is just having a nice sunbathe" I said. Then there was a loud knock at the door. Harry started crying. He didn't want to go, and it took all my energy not to scoop them both up in my arms and not open the door.

I opened the door and James stood there. No smile or acknowledgement of what a big day this was. I tried to reassure Harry, but he was so upset. James took them both by the hand as he had put their baggage in the car and he walked away. As they drove off, Harry and Grace were waving at me from the back window. I felt absolutely devastated. I don't think I had ever felt so lonely in my life!

What if they liked Tracey more than me? All these worries were rushing through my mind. I desperately wanted Grace and Harry to be happy and I had to let them go as James was their father. With that I went into my garage and got a spade. I started digging a big hole to bury Fluffy.

The tears were now streaming, and I could barely see. I was thinking, "one day I will laugh about this". I just couldn't believe that I was burying a dead cat. What the hell had my life become.

Once Fluffy was buried, I got a small overnight bag together and drove off to go and stay with my cousin. She was a single Mum as well, so we were going to spend the night together having a takeaway and wine. As I drove, the tears just kept coming. I felt like someone had reached into me body and ripped my heart out.

The weekend went in a blur. All I could think about was how were Grace and Harry? At 6pm on the Sunday I was home waiting for them. At 5pm Grace and Harry came in. James didn't even stop to tell me how they had been. He just walked off and drove away.

Within minutes both children were crying, and I was cuddling them. I was trying to console them. It had all been too much and they had been as good as gold but now they were home, it was like a release for them. This became a pattern whenever they went to stay overnight.

Due to James job this was usually one night a month but before the children went, they would be clingy and cry at the littlest thing and then when they were dropped, within an hour like clockwork, they had both cried for whatever reason.

Then we would just get back into our own routine and day to day stuff. The problem was that I was sinking financially, and I just didn't know what to do?

Chapter 6 - Rock Bottom and Repossession

The divorce process was coming along nicely, and I had cited adultery as the cause. I chose not to name Tracey because even though I was angry, that wasn't going to solve anything, and I wasn't angry at her. Ultimately, it should've been my husband saying no.

Each day would still start with me trying to prevent a panic attack and breathing into my cupped hands by my toilet. It was almost becoming a second home. It was as much as my daily routine as cleaning my teeth.

I still hated looking at myself in the mirror and would put makeup on and this was my mask. I would go outside the front door and anyone who asked how I was, I would reply with a big smile and a "Fine, thank you." I wasn't going to show that I wasn't coping, even though I wasn't.

Money was a real worry for me because the outgoings were more than the incomings. Then a friend told me that if I put Grace and Harry in a registered childminder's care, I could claim back 80% of my childcare costs! This could give me an extra £100 a month. £25 a week was a lot to me. So, I told my friend Jenny, that Grace and Harry would be going to another childminder and thought she would be pleased for me. She seemed angry at me as was no longer going to be earning £125 a month from me.

I also said to her that my psychotherapist had advised me to stop doing anything for anyone else as I needed to start focusing on my healing and recovery. This seemed to frustrate her even more, and I tried to justify why and explain to her, but it seemed to fall on deaf ears.

My psychotherapist had said to me that even if I put a wash on in the day, that I should see this as an achievement because this to me felt like I was climbing Mount Everest. Everything seemed such an effort, and all I wanted to do was curl up in bed, under my duvet and not see or speak to anyone.

I remember thinking that if I didn't have children, I could have quite happily become agoraphobic. But again, Grace and Harry kept me going. Both were now at school so, during school hours, I would try and do my podiatry and then every Friday I would work late.

My outgoings were still too much each month. I started to avoid any letters that came through the door because I was scared that it was just more bills. I did make sure I paid the council tax though because this was a criminal offence and I certainly did not want to end up in prison.

But all the other letters would come through the door, and I would put in the bin. I just wanted to put my head in the sand. I would call up the utilities each month and pretend that something had happened with my bank account because my card had been cloned and they were always so understanding and would reset up a direct debit the following month so at least, it gave me another month's breathing space.

This became how I lived. I literally would take one day at a time, and some weeks I would have more podiatry appointments and things were marginally better, and then the next week I would be panicking.

My child maintenance was meant to be in my account on the first of each month but more often than not, it would arrive 4 or 5 days late. This meant my direct debits would bounce and so the cycle continued. As I kept checking my bank balance, things were getting worse and worse. I started to panic and thought how was I going to cope?

Harry and Grace were totally oblivious to any of this going on, and the only time there were tears from them, was when they had their overnight stay at their Dad's. Luckily in some respects, this was few and far between as James didn't seem to offer many overnight visits and just said it was his job?

I did find this odd as he worked for a great airline where they got 40 days annual leave and on average ten days at least off every month. I did try to challenge James about this but again, I was shouted down, and he went off on a tangent about something else he could complain to me with.

Then finally our divorce was finalised. James had not put one single penny towards the divorce, and it was my father that had helped me as he now hated James for what he had done and luckily had stopped saying to me to try and patch things up.

I went down to my local court filled with relief. I walked in and went to the desk and asked for my Absolute. It was all so clinical. He   passed it over to me and there in black and white was the end of my marriage. I walked out of the court and crossed the busy road. I found a bench and just sat down staring at the piece of paper before my eyes.

The tears started to flow. I just couldn't stop them. I wasn't crying for the love of my life and that I had lost him, I was crying because of what should have been. When I got married, I had no intention of anything like this ever happening. I had married for life and wanted to have a family and grow old together.

I was crying for the lost future that I no longer felt I had. I had lost my identity and my future was so uncertain now. Who would ever want me now? Who would want a single Mum like me with a huge amount of debt? I felt lonely and a real sense of sadness.

Again, I wished my Mum was alive so that I could have driven straight to her to fall into her arms and for her to hold me and tell me, it would all be ok. Everyone I seemed to have loved was no longer with me.

I got up and went back to my car and went home. The children were going to their Dad's that weekend and again in the build-up the night before, we had tears and Grace would often sleep walk. In the morning as they drove away, I sat down in my lounge and thought about my life. I thought was this as good as it was going to get? I needed to do something about my finances but what?

I looked online to get an idea of what I would get for the house if I sold it? It was in negative equity and then with solicitors' fees and estate agents' fees on top, I was in a hopeless situation. I felt trapped! I couldn't even afford to sell my house. Even if I did, where would I live? What could I afford?

As I was looking online, a free government ran debt company came up and I jotted the number down to call on the Monday. I felt so low and out of control. I started to think that if I could just financially get Grace and Harry to eighteen, then I have given them the start they need. Maybe not the life I envisaged, but I could not have loved them anymore and our bond with each other was even stronger than it was. Before I knew it, I was sat waiting for them on the Sunday. As the car pulled in, Harry and Grace raced out of the car into the house.

James just put their bag on the doorstep and left. He never seemed to want to chat on the doorstep which suited me as I always felt so nervous when he was there, and he seemed much happier in arguing with me in text. The children came running in and gave me a big hug and both started shouting at me.

I couldn't understand what they were saying and asked them to calm down. "Daddy is engaged and he is getting married next month." My heart sank. Not because I was in love with my ex-husband, but we had only just got our absolute the day before and I was so concerned about what message this was sending to our children.

Both in how a man treats a wife but also for my daughter about how a man treats women in general. I was so angry. How dare James not tell me so that at least I would have been prepared for when the children came home? It was like he deliberately wanted me to find out like this and then must deal with the aftermath.

I asked Harry and Grace how they felt. They didn't like Tracey and said they didn't want to go their wedding. I tried to get them to see that I didn't mind them going as Mummy just wanted them to be happy and it would be a fun day, I am sure. But they were adamant.

It was almost like their Dad had taken one step too far, too soon. I tried to change the subject and focus on something fun as I always did when they got dropped off, yet again there were tears.

James text me the following day to tell me Grace and Harry were going to the wedding. I tried to explain that they were both really upset and at that point in time, were not wanting to go to the wedding and that I would try and persuade them.

None of this seemed good enough and I was accused of lying and the children did want to go. I almost wanted to record the children crying and so James could hear what they had said, but this was against my better judgement and I did not want the kids to get in the middle of the fight between me and their Dad. They did not deserve that, and I would do anything in my power to protect them.

The next day, I called the debt agency and explained my circumstances. They could not have been nicer to me. They took all the details of my debts and the mortgage company and said they would talk to them all for me. Relief swept over me because I finally felt like I was doing something. Maybe it would be ok?

I don't really know what I thought they would do but for a few days, I felt like maybe a corner was turning. When they called me back, all the creditors had been helpful and even my mortgage company had said they could reduce my payments but as I looked at all the figures in black and white it wasn't enough. I started to google bankruptcy and repossession.

What if I just handed the keys back? I had tried for months to talk to James about how I was really struggling financially but he just didn't care. It was like he had his new life and that was all that mattered to him. I always felt like I was on the back foot and having to defend myself and yet I was the one with most of the time and they were so happy and content at home in our usual routine.

Visits were erratic and never any continuity, so this always unsettled the children as none of us could ever get in a routine. Every month, I would be messaging asking him for the dates he wanted to see the children, then there would be long gaps and then a text with maybe one overnight and a couple of after school visits. He used his job all the time still as excuses. I just felt sad for Grace and Harry and then I would try and make it up to them all the time.

As James' wedding drew closer, I kept asking the kids to go and they were just both adamant they would not. James stopped asking in the end and on the day of their wedding it felt so strange. That my ex-husband had now remarried someone else?

I didn't know how to feel? Should I feel sad? Should I feel happy? There was a part of me that felt sad. A part of the fact, that marriage was for life. I still had that voice that said I was a failure for having a divorce. Even the word divorce had such a negative association because it meant broken home, single mum and alone. Harry and Grace did not even want to talk about it, so I just let it be.

I started to really research repossession and what this would mean to me long term. The biggest impact was the damage to my credit rating. But I had no credit anyway so that would be no great loss. So, I started to save the mortgage payments as I knew I would need a lump sum to rent. I tried to talk to James but before we could even get to talk about it, he was moaning at me about one thing or another.

I started to look online to see if there were any rental properties close by. I sat and told my Dad what I was doing and as much as he wanted to help me, we both knew that this was the only option and I needed to be in control of it, rather than just to keep going and then it happens when I have no money at all.

I asked on Facebook if anyone knew of any local rentals and

said it was for a friend, and would you believe but my next door but one neighbour had a rental house on the estate where I was already living.

I called him up and asked him if I could go and look at it. I went to look the next day and the moment I walked in, I felt like a big weight was being lifted. It was a three-storey semi-detached and much smaller than my four-bed detached I was in, but it felt calm and free of negative energy.

I just knew we could be happy there. So, I asked him for all the paperwork but there was a sticking point. My credit was rubbish and he needed a credit reference and I knew I would fail. So, I told him my story about divorce and the debt and said he asked if I could get a guarantor as that would be fine.

I went home and called my Dad and asked him and he said yes. I could just about afford the rent in this house and pay the bills. A few months passed whilst I was waiting to move in and in that time, I stopped paying the mortgage.

James didn't have a clue but every time I had ever tried to talk to him about money, all I got was "I give you what the government tell me I have to give you, so it's up to you what you do with it". He just didn't seem bothered at all what happened to me or the kids. It was like he did what he thought he should to show the world he was a good father as his image was so important to him.

But he just seemed to want to be aggressive to me and I was getting tired of all the battles and it was making me ill. I just wanted a fresh start. I knew James wouldn't contribute to the estate agent's fees or solicitors, so he gave me no choice. So, one Tuesday morning, I dropped the kids off at school and they were actually very excited as they were to have the two bedrooms on the third floor.

I came home, and I had two great friends who then helped me move to my new home. By late afternoon, all the boxes had been moved and I was trying to get the lounge and the kids bedrooms sorted so that when I picked them up from school, it felt like our new home.

I put the keys to my old home in an envelope and addressed it to the mortgage company and went to the post office and sent special delivery.

In that moment, I think it was at my lowest point. I had lost my Mum, my husband and now my home in the space of 2 years. Three major traumatic life events that had happen to me in a row within a short timescale and I had just moved to a new house.

I sat in my car crying and feeling so ashamed that I was a failure. Life was meant to become more financially secure as you got older, but I was going backwards. I had nothing. No savings, no house, I was literally living hand to mouth.

I literally only told a few friends and my Dad and sisters what I had done, but I am sure it soon got around to everyone. I am sure the gossipers on the estate where I lived were loving it and I even remember thinking at that time, I should write a book about this because no one would believe me!

I felt like everyone would be looking at me thinking it was all my fault and I wanted to shout and scream that it wasn't. I was doing the best I could under the circumstances. I didn't really know anyone at that time where I lived that had been through a divorce other than a friend of mine and I had seen how badly it affected her and she got regular maintenance and came out of it with a house. I had come out of my marriage with nothing but a great big debt.

James wanted the divorce but wouldn't pay anything towards

it and he was driving my solicitor mad as sending her these hand scrawled replies that she could hardly read. She never minced her words with what she thought of him.

As school pick up time was fast approaching, I wiped away my tears and tried to make myself look half way presentable. When I picked Harry and Grace up, they were both excited. I genuinely never wanted any of this to affect them.

I had been brought up in a happy childhood, both parents together, and whilst we never had any money, I never seemed to want for anything. I just wanted the same for Harry and Grace, but I felt like such a failure. We had a broken home!

I hated that phrase as it was so negative, and I didn't want the stigma of single Mum and a broken home. It made me feel a failure and that I had let my children down. As we drove the other direction to get to our new home, I looked at Harry and Grace all so innocent with what looked like they did not have a care in the world.

We arrived at our new home and the kids raced upstairs to their new bedroom. They were shouting and screaming in delight. I put the kettle on and finished making the lounge look homely and started to think maybe this is a new and fresh start for us?

I went back into the kitchen and started to build a kitchen table. It was always important for me to eat with the children and as a family so that we could keep our strong bond there and we needed a much smaller table in this house. I got all the pieces out of the box and sat and built it. I felt so proud of myself.

This home was much smaller, but it already felt much happier. it felt like the end of a bad chapter and the beginning of a new one. As I went to bed that night, I looked out of the window up at the sky and saw a shooting star. I thought maybe that is my Mum looking down on me and saying she loves me.

She always said bide your time and you will know when the time is right to leave. Now although I never left James, the time was right when we split up. I knew at some stage, I was going to get the wrath of James about moving and sending the keys back to the mortgage company.

We settled into our new home well. The following week, James was seeing the children at the weekend. The night before, I text James and said that he needed to pick the children up from my new address. He went ballistic at me.

I told him that he never listened to me whenever I said anything and just continued to bully me all the time. I was learning to start sticking up for myself, but this just seemed to fuel James more. It was like he was berating me for what I had done, but not willing to do anything to help.

As hard as I tried to be civil and amicable, it was always to no avail. He clearly wanted to keep controlling me and taking digs at me all the time and I felt like this was a bit of fun for him.

When he brought the children back from the weekend, he came to the front door and this time he shouted at me. I ushered the kids into the lounge and went out to speak to him.

But I couldn't get a word in. I said I had tried to see if he would help me more and see the kids more and he was always full of excuses. I felt more like a widow with the amount of time he saw Harry and Grace. He was always constantly chipping away at my confidence and every text he sent had to be an essay about so many different things and if I ever asked him anything, the conversation would divert to me again.

It was just like when we lived together. If he knew he had been caught out or he was in the wrong, he would just change the subject. I was tired of it as I just couldn't co parent with him as much as I kept trying.

My cousin, my friend and my sister all tried to mediate for me and initially as James wanted to make a good impression, all would seem fine but then he would get abusive to them and they refused to converse with him. Even my cousin sat with him one day for half an hour to tell him to back off me and see the kids more and she came back saying, "I think I have got through to him, he said he is going to make more effort and lay off you."

I looked at her and was not convinced. I knew James and knew this was just one of his many tactics to try and look good to others. He had a habit of saying what he thought the other person wanted to hear and would then never follow through. Within four days, my cousin sent me a message. "Well, that was a waste of time. You were right! He just won't let it go about you Caroline and just wants to keep bullying you."

Why couldn't he just leave me alone, see the kids regularly and get on with his own life. I kept wondering why he wanted to keep in contact so much? If he spent as much time as he did trying to text me and saw the children, then that would be a breakthrough.

No one seemed to want to mediate for me because he wore them down as well. I just kept thinking how am I going to cope like this until the children are eighteen? I felt like I was still in a permanent state of anxiety and it was now two years later and I was still angry at James, not so much for our marriage but for how he felt it was acceptable to keep treating me like this.

I was the mother of his children. Why was there no softness? He knew what I was like with the children and he knew I was trying and Harry and Grace were doing so well. The only time they were ever upset was when they spent the night down with their Dad. Every time the children came home, there was always some drama and the kids would be upset.

Their wedding had come and gone, and James asked once more for Harry and Grace to go. I asked them again and they both got upset and said they didn't want to. I explained to James that I would keep trying but I just got shouted and blamed as to why they wouldn't go, and he never asked again.

It was like he could use me all the time as a convenient excuse as to why he didn't see Grace and Harry very much so that he could still look the epitome of a good father and blame the wicked ex-wife. I often wished he could see how hard I tried to get the children to see him and want to be with him, but I think the lack of effort he had put in for the six months following our breakup, was all starting to come back and bite him on the bum.

I was an easy target as to the reason why. I often wondered what would have happened after we broke up, if I hadn't kept on pushing him to see the children? Would he have just stopped altogether for a while? Thoughts like that made me so cross because I never ever wanted Grace or Harry to feel anything else other than totally loved and secure.

I think they knew that I was their rock and security and whilst that meant the world to me, I also felt that pressure. But knowing how I felt with my PTSD and depression, anxiety and harming myself, it was probably a good thing because it gave me that one purpose in life.

We soon settled into our new home and whilst we had no extra money at all, we were happy and content in our home.

We started to make new memories as a three. I felt so lucky to have such wonderful children and I loved them so much I thought my heart would burst.

One evening after I tucked Harry and Grace in bed, I went to my bedroom and lay on my bed and got my phone out. I went on Facebook and I had an icon on my phone that I had never seen? I clicked it and it said it was an "others" folder.

In there I saw lots of messages that people had sent me who were not my friends on Facebook. One stood out to me. It said, "Dear Caroline, I just had to write to you after I read your article in the magazine as I felt so sorry for you and what James had done. He did the same to me and I am so sorry you are going through this." I looked at the name and was from James first wife Claire.

The message had been sent over a year ago. I started to type back apologising for the late response, but I had not seen the message. I told her we had now split up and I lived on my own with our two children. She immediately replied and got chatting. We ended up exchanging numbers and started a chat on the phone.

We hit it off straight away and chatted for over an hour. She told me how James had been the same to her with lies and cheating and that they had only been married 6 months and he walked out. She was just so grateful they didn't have children. She said it took her over 5 years to get over the hurt and pain he had caused.

We both found great comfort in each other and became friends. She still knew people that had been flying with James and that he was always saying at work that he had to do everything at home and take care of the children. I could not believe it as this was so far from the truth.

I loved being a Mum but it all made sense that James wanted to come across as the hard done to husband and a great father to garner sympathy and feed his need for approval and acceptance.

We both had such similar stories although Claire was shocked when I told her mine. We promised to stay connected and remained friends on Facebook.

However, I felt such sadness that my children didn't really have any extended family. One of my sisters was in America and the other one was a teacher, so we rarely saw her as she lived over an hour away. My Dad was in his late seventies and whilst we saw him regularly, my Dad is not the most emotional of people and whilst he was great helping me practically and financially, there was no emotional support from anyone.

I had stopped seeing the psychotherapist as I had no money. I tried seeing a counsellor at my doctors, but I just didn't click with him and he seemed a bit out of his depth with counselling me. James' parents never made any contact with me at all. In fact, to this day, they have never seen Grace and only met Harry twice and the last time was when Harry was four months old. I think they were always more interested in their cats!

It explained a lot as to how James was when I looked at his parents because they had never really made any effort, even when we were married, and they only lived three hours away.

It was so sad as my childhood was very much with our extended family of grandparents and cousins and I used to love our Christmases and parties as we would play games and just be a family. Grace and Harry didn't have any of that. I felt sad for them. I wanted to be the Dad, gran, cousins and best Mum ever to them. I know that this was putting a lot of pressure on myself, but I just couldn't bear them ever to feel anything less than amazing.

Soon people began to realise that I had had my home repossessed. It seemed strange as so many people seemed to know my business and I didn't know where they were getting it all as I was a very private person and only told a few people.

I felt like everyone was laughing at me, that they all thought that I was a failure. I wanted to scream and shout at them and say, "See how you would cope losing your Mum, your marriage and your home." It astounded me that people seemed to not want to look me in the eye, that I was like some leper or something because of what had happened. I felt like I was somehow frowned upon because I was now a single Mum.

It hurt me so much as I kept thinking that I would never be like that to anyone else. I know it was probably partly my fault because I would put my make up on each day, to hide behind a mask and then I would walk out the front door with a big smile. "How are you, Caroline?", "I am great," I would reply". What I really wanted to say was scream and shout "I am not okay, I am sad and lonely and feel like such a failure!"

But who would care anyway? Everyone was getting on with their lives. I had my small circle of friends and my best friend I would confide in. But if I am honest, I just didn't want to keep burdening people with my problems. The only good thing was that my panic attacks were getting less being in the new house.

I was still suffering with anxiety as I would wake up every day with pins and needles, but my depression seemed to have lessened and my panic attacks seemed to have calmed down.

The most stressed I would get would be when I would see a

text from James and know that it would be some bullying of some kind and that it wouldn't be a conversation, but a conflict and argument.

Whenever James had to pick him up from the house, I would be so anxious beforehand, and would desperately try and hide it from the children as there was usually some dig at me.

Once the kids had gone, I would have an actual physical reaction and start shaking. It was like I feared him as it always seemed such a battle and just continued to wear me down.

When would I ever feel better again?

Chapter 7 - Hope in The Darkness

We were now all settled into our new home and had a bit of a routine in place. The children were at school and both loved our local primary school. I would get James dates for wanting to see the children usually around mid-month, if not later for the following month even though I knew when he got his roster as he always seemed to forget that I worked for the same airline years previously and knew exactly when the following months roster came out.

It always astounded me that he didn't send them immediately to me so that he could secure time with the children, but I was learning that this was not to be the case. I wondered if he was deliberately sending them later because this made it so difficult for me to ever plan anything as I genuinely wanted the children to see their Dad, but I couldn't make him.

The more I tried, the more abuse I got. Even his wife would message me abuse but at the end of the day, I recognised that she was only ever going by what James said, but I would never get involved like she was as it was not her place. I even wondered at various times if James was regretting leaving me?

Or was it just that he wanted to still hold on to controlling the situation? Life felt like I was walking in treacle and never really moving forward. I would just think I was on the road to healing when we would have another big row about something.

I would try and defend myself and smooth the situation over because I hated conflict. I have always hated arguing and I am a real nurturing person, so I will always try and make sure everyone else is happy and very often to my own detriment.

I was working hard as a podiatrist, but we still seemed to never have any money. What with rent, bills, food and clothes. James gave me what he had to each month but even with all that, I was still struggling.

If the kids started to get poorly mid-week, I would be dosing them up and giving them vitamin C because I knew if I couldn't work on Friday, I would get zero money as I was self-employed and that meant no food money for the following week.

This happened on several occasions where they were both too ill to go to school, so I had to look after them. The following week was always so hard because I would make sure Grace and Harry were fed and I would live on toast or my sweet chilli Snack-a-Jacks!

The only good thing about all the stress I had been under is that I had lost a lot of weight and I was exercising more. In fact, I was becoming almost obsessional about exercise because it gave me a release rather than harming myself which had greatly reduced by this stage. In fact, it was only really my anxiety that I was still really struggling to control.

One day whilst I was having my daily bath, I checked my breasts as I often checked myself and I found a lump. The lump was like a small apricot and under my left armpit. My heart sank, and I started to think about the worse.

What if I had cancer? What if I had to have radiotherapy and chemotherapy? Who would look after Grace and Harry? The thought of them living with James turned my stomach as I knew they wouldn't want to go there. What if, even worse, I died? They would have to go and live with their Dad permanently and the whole thought made me so fearful and fill up with tears.

My Auntie, my Mum's sister, had died 10 years earlier of breast cancer, so I knew the devastating effects of this awful disease. As I kept touching the lump, I tried to calm myself down and think what I was going to do.

I needed to call the doctor first thing in the morning and see him. So, I got out of the bath and dried myself and went to my bedroom to watch TV and try and take my mind of it. I felt my anxiety soar through the roof because I had to be there for my children. I was their rock. I was their security blanket. I was their soft place to fall. I fell asleep exhausted at gone 2am.

The next morning, once I had dropped the children at school and I was at home, I called the doctor and made an appointment. I sat nervously in the waiting room waiting to go in. "Caroline Strawson" called the doctor and I got up and went into the room with him.

I explained what I had found, and about my family history and he said that he would write a letter of referral to the hospital and I would be seen by the breast care clinic there. I asked how long I would need to wait and he said two weeks maximum.

Two weeks seemed like an eternity as every day I would be running through scenarios of what if I had cancer, what if I needed treatment, how would the bills be paid, who would look after Grace and Harry and what if I died. I had never feared death before because I almost thought I was invincible, but I think because of the last few years, I suddenly felt vulnerable and alone.

My appointment came through from the hospital and I went down there on my own. I saw the consultant and he was a lovely man and tried to reassure me that the likelihood was that it was not anything serious. I went into the X-Ray room and had a mammogram. He felt my lump and asked me more questions.

He informed me that I had excess accessory breast tissue and was fine and that over time, I may see the lump get bigger around my cycle and go down again. I asked if there was anything I could do as it was by now quite a big lump and he just informed me that there is an operation but maybe not the right time for you yet.

I left the hospital feeling drained and thankful. It was just excess breast tissue. Yay, I had an extra boob! I couldn't even go home and tell a partner and have a good giggle but at least I was going to be OK. The consultant was right because over the coming weeks, the lump did start to go down.

This all made me look more at my life, my finances and what I was doing with them. My 40th birthday was coming up and I didn't mind getting older, but it was a stark reminder of what my life was like. I organised a night out with my friends on my birthday and got my Dad to babysit but was home early.

I felt emotional and just wanted to be home with my children. I felt like whenever I went out, people would stare and think about what a failure I was. This was all in my head but it all really affected me. As the weeks were going by, I kept evaluating my life.

I thought back to when I was in my early twenties. I was fiercely ambitious and whatever I put my mind to, I wanted to excel at. I had always been a high achiever at school and played county sports.

I had been picked to do promotional work for the airline I had worked at and the CEO was such an inspiration to me and I met him on many occasions whilst doing lots of promo work. I was in adverts in magazines and newspapers.

Then, when I worked for the next airline, I was personally picked from over 12,000 cabin crew to be part of an elite team of cabin crew to carry the Royal family and the then Prime Minister.

I remember being in New York just days after September 11th and it was one of the most horrific and moving days I have ever experienced. I remember walking down to Ground Zero and just standing there trying to get my head around the events of the last week. It all looked like a film set, with big lights everywhere and the smell of ash filled the air. There were posters everywhere of lost relatives and there was an eerie silence around the area. I stood there and said a quiet prayer for all the lost loved ones and prayed that they would still maybe find any more survivors.

When I got home from the trip, I remember that I just cried in James' arms. He wasn't chosen for the special flights and it was one of the only times we didn't fly together. The trip had made me realise that life is precious, and it truly changed my outlook in that moment. The following months the airline I was working for asked if anyone wanted any unpaid leave.

I had been spotted on a trip down to Australia by a man I was serving in First Class as he asked me if I had ever thought about shopping telly. I thought he was crazy and coming on to me but as we chatted, I realised he was serious. I was only 27 and I was someone who loved adventure and opportunity, so I ended up being flown to Los Angeles and doing some infomercials for his company.

I had a great time and James came with me. I enjoyed it so much. I wondered if I could do this for real back home, so I bought a newspaper that had all things like this in and the second largest shopping channel in the UK was looking for presenters.

Dare I apply? So, I sent my video off to them of my infomercials and the following week I got a call for an interview. Excited and nervous, I turned up at the interview.

My heart was racing but I loved a challenge and I wanted to do the best I could. I quickly realised that I was hugely out of my depth as there were radio presenters there and other shopping channel presenters, and then there was me! I went in to see the panel of interviewers and had to pretend to sell them some face cream. I just decided to go for it.

As the day progressed and they were sending more and more people home, I was still there! I couldn't quite believe it, but I was giving it my best shot! Then, as the day was ending, they called me in to the interview room. They loved me! They said that they could tell I was very inexperienced, but they would love to train me and have me as one of their live presenters.

Had I heard that right? They were offering me the job? I said yes and thought I would sort the details out later and drove home.

My Mum had been so right. Put your mind to anything, Caroline, and you can do it. The airline was offering unpaid leave at the time, so I took that and worked for the shopping channel for 6 months. I really enjoyed it, but the only problem was that I never saw James as he was still flying. So, at the end of my 6 months unpaid leave, I had to make a decision and I chose to return to flying.

Wow, I really had been independent, full of life and ambitious back then. As I sat there, I started to cry because I knew that I had completely lost myself now. I wasn't like this anymore. The brave and ballsy Caroline that would go for everything and strive to the top seemed like a distant memory.

Maybe I was not that woman anymore and the sooner I accepted that the better. But there was something inside of me that just kept on saying "don't you dare give up." But I looked at my bank account and often there would literally be pence in it. I think the lowest I got was 42p. I didn't even have any credit cards because of my debt and I didn't have an overdraft. What I had was what I had.

But how could a single Mum with no money ever get out of this tax credit trap that I was in? I couldn't do anymore hours because that meant I would need more childcare and the school holidays would just wipe out what I was learning.

What could I do? Again, I found myself thinking that if I could just get them to eighteen and focus on one month at a time and I would somehow get through it?

James had always said when we split up that he would pay for half the uniforms and half the school trips. Both Grace and Harry had got some days out for their school, so I asked James for half like he promised to give me. It had taken me so much courage to ask him and I had spent days building up to it because I was scared that he would just shout at me and say no.

He didn't quite say no, but he did say, "I give you child maintenance what the government say I have to give you so it's up to you what you do with it." I tried to say that he had promised, and he just walked away. Grace and Harry were hearing all of this and whilst I never bad mouthed their father in front of them, they knew we did not get on, but I had explained to them that our love for them was very different and I knew they would form their own opinions anyway.

Harry already had asked me why his Dad lied all the time. James had promised Harry so much when he left like he would move back closer and see him all the time. None of this had transpired and Harry had such a good memory that he never forgot anything.

They both loved their Dad, but they were both starting to form their own opinions and however much I even tried to explain why their father was like that or why he hardly saw them, they were making their own assumptions. I was still trying to make excuses for him.

I think James thought I always bad mouthed him and was trying to cause problems, but I genuinely wasn't. I was only ever going by how Grace and Harry were and then trying to make the situation as agreeable for everyone. It just seemed like James always thought I was the bad guy. I would often say to my Dad that I wished James could hear how I try so desperately to get them to call their Dad or be less upset about going but I think I was destined to be blamed for everything.

I just think it suited James' facade that he lived where he could give excuses for why he wasn't seeing the children very much because he had a wicked ex-wife. I am sure many of his friends believed him but there are two sides to every story and I know how convincing James could be.

After all, I was married to him for 12 years and when I looked back at all the lies, it scared me to death as I did not know what was real in our marriage and what wasn't. I am sure there is also so much I did not even know.

I was feeling exhausted. I was working as much as I could, looking after Grace and Harry and never really getting any break. I was constantly thinking why me? Why was all this bad stuff happening to me? When was something good going to happen?

I wanted a knight in shining armour on a big white horse to come in and rescue me and tell me everything was going to be OK. I was in for a long wait as there was no sign of any knight. I knew if I wanted my life to change, then I needed to change. I needed to stop being a victim of my circumstances.

My lump under my arm was painful and I remembered a woman I had met at an event I did years previously who was selling these products and she had a deodorant that had no aluminium in and my consultant had advised me to use one without this in. I looked her up on Facebook and could see that she was running a business from home around her children. So, I dropped her a Facebook message about the deodorant and the business.

She only lived 15 minutes away from me so she offered to come around for a coffee and tell me more and bring my deodorant. As I sat waiting for her, something inside me changed. What if this was my plan B? What if I could do what she was doing? What if this was something where I could earn a bit of extra money? I could start to feel a little flutter in my tummy. What if this was my answer?

Helen arrived at my house and came in. She had brought the deodorant for me and began to tell me about the business. All I heard was use products, recommend them and you can do this from home. I'm in, I heard myself say out loud. But there was a sticking point.

To get started I needed to buy a box of products so that I could use them and build credibility and that made sense as selling products I had never used, I thought no one will believe me. It was just under £200 to start. I had nothing! I told Helen I was going to ask my Dad if he would lend me the money as I was suddenly excited.

Helen said I could earn an extra £200 a month and for me the thought of an extra £50 a week was so exciting as this was a lot of money for me. So, when Helen left, I drove around to my Dad's. He was so sceptical but I told him that the box of products had everything in that I would have to buy over the next few months anyway, like shampoo and conditioner, and I told him that this was the only thing I could think of doing that still enabled me to carry on with my podiatry and earn a bit of extra money around Harry and Grace. He could see how desperate I was, so he lent me the money.

I went home, called Helen and ordered the box. I had just started a home-based business! I was so excited and started to read everything I could about the products. I wanted to be the best student I could be, and I desperately wanted to earn that extra few hundred pounds.

A few days later the box arrived, and it was like Christmas. I had a nice bath and tried all the products. I loved them all. I had always been a product junkie ever since I was a child and I was always cleansing or moisturising or something! So, it was no surprise to my sisters that I was doing this.

I had some friends around for an evening where we all had a play with the products and some of my friends bought some. I think they just felt sorry for me, really, but it was exciting to think that I was starting to have some hope in life as it had long felt like a dark tunnel with no light at the end of it.

As the weeks passed, I was loving using the products and was getting a lot of personal benefit out of them and all of a sudden got a promotion in my business. Within two weeks of starting I had paid my Dad back. Within in four weeks I was earning that extra £200 a month that I so desperately needed.

However, within the company there were many people earning way more than that and I thought how? So, I started to study and learn what they were doing. Slowly, my confidence was starting to increase, and I could see my life getting better.

James was still being aggressive and it always still really affected me, so I would tell my small circle of friends about what he was doing and how I was feeling. The following months I suddenly started to get negativity surrounding what I was doing from home. I don't even know why because I am not into hard sales, so I would never ask anyone to buy from me. I would let them ask me.

One of my daughter's school friends took me to one side to say that she had overheard my best friend slating the products and being really negative. I was so hurt and shocked. Surely she could see that this was making me happy since I was finally getting a bit of control back in my life? Why wasn't she pleased? I didn't say anything but this all made me start to question whether I was doing the right thing.

It seemed me doing something different where I lived was causing a bit of unease as they hadn't seen anyone do what I was doing and doing well. But was it worth it? I hated any conflict and hated anyone thinking badly of me, so I really started to question myself if I was doing the right thing.

I had then had a phone call from one of my patients who I knew well, and she told me that she just had to phone me to tell me something. "What?" I asked. She went on to tell me that Helen was telling everyone my personal details and constantly gossiping about my life. I knew Jenny was a gossip because whenever we met up, she would always have something to say about this person and that person, but I suppose I just kind of trusted her.

I remember when I had told her that I couldn't look after her children and then after six months, she asked me as a one off could I look after them and I felt OK to say yes, that she told me "Gosh, you went all selfish there for a while." Again, I just took it. I started to think was there a pattern in the type of people I attracted into my life as I always seemed to give my all, but it never seemed enough.

Even knowing this about her gossiping from a patient, I still never said anything. Anything to avoid conflict. Then, one day when James dropped Grace and Harry home, James said something to me that I knew I had only ever told Jenny. My heart stopped, and I thought that this was the final straw. But rather than going around to Jenny's, I just sent a text to my three friends and said I was stepping away from the friendship group as I did not want to cause an argument. Again, I was still so wounded from my marriage that I did not want any type of confrontation.

Within 15 minutes, Jenny was banging on my door. I hid in my lounge. I just did not know what to say to her because I knew she would lie or deny it, but I knew the truth. I didn't want to speak to another human that was prepared to lie to my face. I had enough of that.

As I thought about my business, I thought am I really going to give up my business, hopes and dreams for a bit of negativity? I could see how well people were doing in the business and I knew if they could do it, I could do it. So, that is exactly what I did.

Within 7 months, I had doubled my podiatry salary and I decided to leave so that I could be at home all the time and sack the childminder. I could now go to all the kids' events and never miss anything. Due to my anxiety, I didn't build my business the traditional way, I built it using Facebook.

Facebook became my best friend and I studied long hours learning how to master the platform and use it to build my business. Within the year, I was completely debt free. I couldn't believe it!

I worked so hard and often I was up early and went to bed late, but I was always there dropping my children at school and picking them up. I was qualifying for all these amazing free holidays to Singapore, South Africa and Cancun! There were even thousands of pounds worth of bonuses.

I decided to enrol my eldest son into private secondary school because my business was just going from strength to strength. Within two years, my business was turning over more than £1 million worth of products and I was speaking in large arenas of 3000 plus people. I couldn't believe it.

My ex was the only blot on the landscape. He was still wanting to argue all the time and seemingly never stop the conflict. I remember going to the petrol station one day and filled the tank up with petrol until the car was full and I just had tears streaming down my face because I could not believe it.

In the darkest days, Grace and Harry would pick up coins from the floor and rather than keeping them like most children would, they would give them to me. I was investing heavily in myself and self-development was becoming a huge part of my life.

I was listening to YouTube, going to events when I could, reading books and listening to CD's in the car. I was literally feeding my mind. All my little steps that I was doing were all turning into giant leaps. When James picked up the children, the thought that I was earning more than him and his wife put together now always made me smile inside. He knew I was struggling with time and not once had he ever offered to help.

It was always left to me. I was finally starting to let go of my anger. To feel that I was financially back in control. My credit rating was still poor, but I could even see that start to go up.

I still hadn't spoken to Jenny. Maybe she knew the reason why, and knew that if she asked then she would have to admit it, so she never even tried to make it up with me. I used to hear that Jenny and James would chat in the school playground and that made me so sad because Jenny had known how tough I had found everything, and the thought of her telling James made me feel sick.

I realised that both Jenny and James had never truly given me anything that wasn't going to benefit them in some way. I thought about that when both got found out that they were lying, backed away and tried to cover it all up rather than admit anything and apologise.

Why was I attracting people like this into my life? Why couldn't I attract someone who was like me, loyal and trustworthy? However, not being around a gossip was also kind of liberating because women can be so cruel to each other and I realised that I didn't want to around anyone or anything toxic because I was still on my very own fragile healing journey.

I focused on looking after Grace and Harry and ensuring that I was working hard in my business and the beauty of it was I could do it all from my phone or laptop! I developed a system to help my team on how they could also build a business like mine from home all from Facebook and it was exciting seeing my team start to quit their jobs too.

It felt good to be earning my own money, be debt free, no longer on any tax credits and I could now finally open letters that came through the door because I knew I had the money to pay the bills.

The weight that had been lifted was amazing. I was meeting so many new people online and helping them and as my confidence grew, I even started to dip my toe into face to face networking where I live.

This was massively out of my comfort zone but an amazing lady who was running a local lady only group helped and supported me to build my confidence. Life was finally starting to get better, but I was lonely and felt that there was one thing missing. To dip my toe back into the dating scene.

Chapter 8 - Who Would Ever Want Me Now?

After my divorce had come through, I was so low that the last thing from my mind was ever meeting anyone ever again. Firstly, I felt so disgusting and ashamed, I would think that no one would ever want me now.

I am a single Mum with two young children and hardly the catch of the century. James had made me so wary of all men that I wondered if there were any genuine men out there? I just felt like I had been duped in my marriage and that when I first met James, he seemed so nice and genuine.

This is one of the things that was really bugging me still that I could see James putting on this friendly persona talking to people and bad mouthing me so that he looked better as an ex husband and father. I wanted to follow him around after he had spoken to everyone and I wanted to put my side of the story across. I hated to think that anyone thought I was a bad Mum.

Being a Mum was the most important job in the world to me and one that I took so seriously. I didn't want anyone questioning me or even thinking badly of me. The children were my Achilles heel and James knew this, so he knew how to upset me the most because I would do anything in my power to ensure that the children felt happy, safe and secure.

I felt really cross that James had made me become so mistrusting because I never wanted anyone to hurt me like that again.

How could I have been such a fool and got sucked in. How could I have believed all of this lies. I realised that my anger was beginning to change. I was still angry at James, but I was starting to feel angry at myself. I knew why I had stayed for so long and that was because I wanted Grace and Harry to have a family unit at whatever cost.

The cost had been my happiness, my confidence and my self-worth but my parents never divorced so in my mind's eye this was the ideal family set up. I had done extensive reading on this and all the research was pointing to the fact that it was much better to have two happy parents separately than two unhappy ones married.

I couldn't believe that I had beaten myself up for so long about this because I thought I had failed my children, that I had let them down and that their childhood was ruined and I had to make up for all of that. When in fact, Grace and Harry were two very happy children and we had the most amazing relationship.

Their relationship with their Dad was not what I would have wished but I couldn't control how James behaved. I did find comfort that if I did ever meet anyone else again, they would never have the hold over me like James had as they were my children.

So, I started to think that I would love to meet someone. But where the hell does a woman in her forties meet another man? I was hardly going to meet Mr Right going out clubbing at the weekend! I hadn't been on a date for over 15 years! It scared the hell out of me. What if they were like James and lied?

What if he made me lose everything again? I could never ever go back to that dark place ever again.

I know on several occasions my thoughts had got so dark that it had scared me. It was only knowing that Grace and Harry were reliant on me that it stopped me from doing anything stupid, but I dread to think what I would have done had I not had them. They were my soul saviours.

Also, how was I going to introduce a new man to them? What if they didn't like him like they didn't like Tracey? Was this even going to be worth trying? My cousin was already on an online dating website and I had been asking her lots of questions because I just did not have a clue!

She reeled off all these dos and don'ts and I thought it all seemed so overwhelming and complicated but if I wanted to meet someone then I needed to step out and online did seem to have its advantages in that I didn't have to meet anyone. I could go at my own pace and block anyone who didn't seem very nice.

The first thing I needed to do was take a profile photo of myself. Gosh, this was so hard since I hated taking photos of myself. In fact, I hardly had any of me with the kids growing up as I would rather be the one taking the photo as opposed to being in it. I was still feeling so low about how I looked but I was gradually realising that if I wanted to live a happier life, I needed to take responsibility for that because no one was going to come and rescue me.

So, I put on a nice top and did my hair and makeup and started to try and take some selfies. Turn to the left, turn to the right, smile, don't smile, to pout or not to pout, face and body or a close-up? This was harder than I thought!

What if someone messaged me and was mean and nasty to

me? I am not sure I could have taken that as my confidence was still shaky. I went into my bathroom knowing the light was better in there and moved the phone higher as I got better light and angles then.

Thank you, Tyra Banks from America's Next Top Model, as she had given me some pointers. Over 50 photos' later, I had a few that I thought were half decent. I still looked at them and felt a shiver of how I was still ugly and that I bet no one would message me.

Now, which site was I going to sign up to? Some were paid, and some were free. I read lots of reviews and decided to plump for a free one first and dip my toe in the water. I was both excited and scared all at the same time as this felt like a step forward. I hated being on my own but it had allowed me time to heal and build myself up a bit and I was becoming a lover of positive psychology which is the scientific study of happiness. I wanted to be happy again. I wanted to smile again.

My home-based business was going well, and I felt like meeting someone would be another piece of the jigsaw puzzle. So, I filled in the form and uploaded my photo. I could express areas and things like height. Height was a huge issue for me as I was 5 feet 11 and what if I wanted to wear heels? I would put a 6 feet minimum height down because then at least I would feel like the woman. I didn't want to be taller than a man I dated as I just felt this was not right for me. And send, I was in!

I had signed up to a dating website! What had I done? I started to get the kids' tea ready and I heard my phone ping. I glanced down and saw I had a message. My heart started to pound. Someone had liked me enough to message me! I carried on cooking tea and I kept hearing all these pings coming from my phone. I was excited as maybe there was a nice man waiting at the end of the message, but James was a nice man at first. He said and did all the right things at the start of our relationship.

How would I know if any of these men were like him? Thing was how would I ever know they weren't? I could decide to never meet anyone again or I could recognise that it was scary and be extra vigilant. Once I had tucked the kids in bed, I went and lay on my bed and picked my phone up.

There were 36 messages waiting for me! Was I new fodder on the site and this meant that I would get lots of messages? I opened the first message, "Hey MILF" it started. He was a young guy of 24 and it was a nice message but why was he calling me MILF.

My username was Phoenix as I felt like I was a phoenix rising from the ashes and thought it a cool name. Well, I wasn't going to meet him, but it felt good to have a 24-year-old message me. Onto the next message. "Hi Phoenix," it started. This seemed better and he seemed like a nice guy. However, when I looked at his height, he was 5 feet 6. This was a no go. But what did I say back? Did I say, "Hi, but you are too short"! I hadn't signed up to be mean to anyone else, so I decided my best course of action was to just not reply.

Next message, "How are you, MILF?" What the hell! Why was this guy calling me MILF again? I went back to see if I had put something on my profile about MILF as wondered why these two guys had messaged me that. I couldn't see anything, so I just left it.

Next message, now this one seemed nice. He was over 6 feet, but he lived miles away from me. Now, what did I do? I sent him a reply and we started chatting. I was sat chatting to another man and he seemed nice. He was very complimentary about my photos and said I looked gorgeous. Me? Was he actually talking to me? I was gorgeous? I wanted to type back and say are you sure you mean me?

It was so nice to be spoken to like this as I could not remember when this had happened. We chatted some more and then we said we may catch up the next day.

Next message. "Evening, MILF." Then, not only was this the message but he had sent a photo, too. Oh, my goodness! I looked away and looked back again. It was of his penis! I didn't know whether to block him or laugh. Who in their right mind would send a picture of their penis? Was this supposed to make me think yes, let's meet, you seem a good catch? It did make me laugh, though, and I was enjoying a different focus for a few hours.

The T.V. was on in my bedroom and was I was engrossed in my phone. What was this MILF? That was 3 out the first 4 messages that I had opened. These guys were all in their twenties and I did think why would they want to hook up with me? A woman in her early forties with children?

MILF must mean something, so I googled it. Mums I Would Like to F#@$. Oh, my goodness! I laughed out loud! How naive of me. This just showed how long I had been out of the dating game but although there was no way I was going to date them, it felt good and I started to think maybe I am not that bad? Maybe I am OK? Maybe a man would want to date me and be nice?

As the months progressed, I became more and more savvy at the ins and outs of online dating. I knew when to block, I knew if they were fake profiles and I knew if they were just after sex. I was still getting lots of messages with MILF but that was kind of cool as it was building up my confidence.

There actually seemed to be some nice men out there although some seemed to be really struggling to deal with their own past and lots had also been hurt just like me. I would get lots of messages and this gave me something to do in the evening when the kids were in bed as these were always usually my loneliest times.

It just meant I could have someone to talk to even if I had no intention of ever meeting them. I was messaged by young men, old men, lesbians, transvestites, you name it and I had messages from them. I found it fascinating!

I became good friends with a transvestite as he messaged me asking me how I did my eye make-up! It was a whole new world to me and one that still scared me, but I had ventured out and had a few coffee dates. I met some nice guys but overall, no one I could see having a long-term relationship with. I was still getting loads of photos of men's private parts and I even had one guy send me a short video of himself in the shower!

These all made me laugh and my friends were loving these messages the most. In fact, when we were together, they would grab my iPad and say who's been messaging you and want to have a good read!

One of my friends had only ever been with her husband and she always seemed to have the most interest in the photos. I would see her zooming in and out like she was fascinated with all the different shapes and sizes. We had a good giggle and it was such a lot of fun.

Maybe now wasn't the time to meet Mr Right but maybe I could meet Mr Right Now and simply just have some fun? My life had been no fun for so long and I felt I just wanted to laugh, be treated like a queen and made to feel special.

With a few guys I thought maybe this could go further, but the moment I had any doubts or felt they were trying to start to control me, this was a big red flag to me and I ended seeing him.

One guy messaged me who seemed good. I was getting excited as he was in the police, he was way taller than me and his photos looked great. He seemed to be my ideal match and were getting on great.

We arranged to meet for lunch and that was my first mistake. I had only ever met for coffee before because if it was a disaster, I could leave quickly and no harm was done. The kids were at school and I drove to meet him.

As I arrived, I messaged him that I was there and he said he was as well. We were both parked in the same car park. I got out of my car and I could see him get out of his. As I started to walk closer, my heart sank. He looked very different from his photo? In fact, it looked like his photo could have been of him 10 years ago. He was heavier, and he had adult acne. He even sounded different, but I wasn't sure whether that was just me. He smelt of body odour and I was cringing inside. I could not physically think of anything worse than sitting with this man for lunch. He was being all chatty and enthusiastic and all I could think about was how the hell could I get out of this.

We started walking towards the exit of the car park. My heart was pounding, and I felt my skin was crawling. I reached in my handbag and took out my phone. I looked at my phone, took a deep breath and said, "Oh no! My childminder has just text to say she has my daughter as the school tried calling me and as there was no answer called her as Grace has been sick."

I looked at him and said, "I am so sorry, but I am going to have to go." He asked me to call my childminder and ask if I could be back later and we could just grab a coffee, but I just simply couldn't spend another minute with this man. "I am so sorry but as she has been sick, and my childminder has other children, I need to pick her up as soon as possible." With that, I hastily started to walk back to my car, got in, fastened my seatbelt and drove off.

My heart was pounding, and I called my cousin from the car to tell her what had just happened. We were roaring laughing and whilst I did feel bad for leaving like that, I was also angry that he had lied with his photos. When I arrived back home, I deleted him and blocked him on everything. I didn't want to have any conversation with him as there was no point. Were there any honest, decent men out there that I could meet? As much as I was having fun, I was starting to feel like I was destined to be alone forever.

Then, a guy called Bigfoot messaged me. This was his username and we immediately hit it off. He had children of similar ages and seemed to be normal, whatever normal was.

He seemed kind and caring and genuinely interested in me. He was taller than me and I thought he was good looking with a real sparkle in his eyes. He asked me out on a date and I said yes. There seemed to be something about Sam that was drawing me in. He would text me a lot and just seemed attentive. He genuinely seemed like he wanted to meet me and see what could happen.

On the day of our date, I was nervous. We were meeting in a local Starbucks for a coffee at 11am. I put on a nice cream jumper, jeans and some boots and made an extra effort with my hair and makeup. As I was driving there, I was reflecting on my experience with online dating so far. It seemed rather hit and miss but I was learning some key ways to sift through people and narrow it down.

It was still a godsend for me in the evenings as it allowed me to chat with no strings but still feel like I was not alone. When

I arrived, I parked up and started to walk towards Starbucks. I could see exactly where he was, sat in jeans and a navy jumper and Timberland boots. Yay! He actually looks like his pictures. As I walked closer, Sam got up and gave me a big warm smile. He leant forward and kissed me on the cheek and asked me what I would like to drink.

He ordered our drinks and we sat down and started chatting. I found myself being nervous, but Sam made me relax and we had lots of fun conversation. There were never any awkward silences, the conversation just flowed. We chatted about our previous marriages, our children and what our interests were. We both seemed very similar.

The next thing I knew it was nearly 1pm. Sam looked at me with his blue eyes and asked if I would like to have lunch with him. Now, this was definitely a lunch date I would say yes to and not have any sharp exits. As we got up to walk to a restaurant across the road, Sam took my hand in his and it seemed like the most natural thing in the world. I felt the happiest I had felt in a very long time. I certainly did not want to count my chickens but this was the best date I had been on so far.

We sat and had lunch and at the end Sam offered to pay. I am a real romantic and loved all of this and I could not have wished for a better date. As Sam was walking me back to my car, he asked if he could see me again. I smiled at him and said I would love to and with that he kissed me on the cheek again and said he would message me to arrange.

As the next few months went by, Sam and I saw more and more of each other. We discussed when we would introduce our children to each other as this was a big deal to us. I couldn't remember the last time I felt this happy. I was still very vulnerable, but Sam did everything in his power to make me feel at ease. I was still very guarded and had a wall up, but

Sam was the first guy that I had been with that I could truly see a future with. Soon after, both of us met each other's children. He had three daughters of similar ages to mine and everyone all seemed to get on great.

We started talking about the future more and more and every time this subject came up, half of me was excited, yet the other half was so scared. I was falling more and more for Sam and knew that the risk was getting higher for me to get hurt. I met his parents and he met my Dad. The only negative in my life was James who was still randomly sending me horrible messages.

My Dad kept saying to me just don't read it, but I felt I had to read it because what if it was about Grace and Harry. Once I read it, it was in my head and I needed to defend myself. Every conflict we had was a repeated pattern with him accusing me of something, I would respond and tell him the truth that he already knew and rather than just backing down and admitting it, he would just move onto another subject. It was so tiring!

Sam was great at supporting me with James as he could see how much it still affected me and he could read the texts that he sent me. It felt good having someone on my side finally that was right by my side.

I was still scared of my feelings for Sam as we literally had not had one single argument. In fact, the only cross words we ever had was all down to my insecurity. It made me release how much impact James had been on my mental health and it was still a work in progress. I was like a sponge reading books on self-development and positive psychology as each day, I started to feel that little bit stronger.

I had a great home-based business, I had a fantastic boyfriend and two happy children. It still felt surreal. I felt almost like I didn't deserve to be this happy and really struggled with feeling happy. I realised that feeling sad and angry had become such a part of my life that it was a habit.

I had forgotten how to be happy and just live in the moment. I still got anxious thinking about James picking the kids and I still felt anxious about what the future would hold but still no more depression or self-harm. I am sure when I explained to Sam about my marriage and how badly it had affected me, he must have thought I was crazy.

But when he could see first-hand the messages from James, he understood how hard it was for me to move on as there was always a constant reminder in the background when a text came through or if he dropped them off at my home. I desperately did not want to ruin my relationship with Sam because of my failed marriage to James.

Sam was a completely different man and it was not fair to judge him the same as James as he had done nothing to make me doubt him at all. I needed to separate one man from others as this was not fair. Of course, I did not want to be hurt again but nothing is certain in this life as I found out with my Mum, so I wanted to grab happiness with both hands.

One weekend when Grace and Harry were with their Dad overnight, Sam surprised me with a weekend away in London. I felt so special as I had forgotten what it was like to be treated like a woman and someone special.

I packed my weekend bag and got the train into London. He had booked a hotel right in Leicester Square and we dropped our bags and went for lunch. It was all so romantic, and I felt like I would burst with happiness. As were having lunch, Sam surprised me with tickets to go and see The Lion King. I had always wanted to see that, and it brought tears to my eyes. I loved the film and always cried, and the music was so powerful.

After lunch, we headed to the theatre and watched the show. It was amazing. I almost felt bad that I was seeing this and not my children, but I kept thinking I need to teach my children that Mummy can be happy when they are not with me because I did not want to put them under pressure that it was their responsibility to make me happy.

That night, we went to a lovely restaurant and when we got back to our hotel room, Sam scooped me in his arms and told me that he loved me. Me? Sam loved me? Tears sprang to my eyes as I couldn't believe it. I had so many emotions going through my brain as I replied, "I love you, too." Part of me was so happy and the other part was petrified. I had loved James and look what he did? Could I really love another man and him not hurt me? So many what ifs?

It was the best weekend. We went for breakfast in Covent Garden and there was never any shortage of conversation. At lunchtime, we packed our bags and got the train home. It had been one of the best weekends I could remember, and I knew in that moment I would never forget it.

As I sat waiting for the kids to get home that night, I sat waiting filled with excitement and happiness. I could feel my life turning around and although I still had moments of doubt and vulnerability, I knew I needed to realise that my life and my happiness was in my control. Not James', or my children's or Sam's. I realised that the biggest gift I could give myself was to release the anger I was holding onto.

Over the next few weeks, Sam and I saw more and more of each other. Grace and Harry got on like a house on fire with him and that was such a relief to me. Often, on a weekend, we would take all five children on a day trip to places like Warwick Castle or the Natural History Museum. We felt like the Von Trapp family from the Sound of Music. Life was good. As time went on, Sam and I just grew stronger and stronger.

My home-based business was going from strength to strength and finally my finances were in a state that I had never seen them. My credit score was still low because of the debt and repossession but I could see it move from very poor to poor and now it was good. I was getting there, slowly but surely.

Every day I felt stronger and felt myself going back to the old me. In fact, it wasn't even a case of the old me. It was a better, stronger me because of what I had been through. I was loving my business and working as hard as ever. I never doubted my own work ethic.

I was meeting so many women and so many had been through or were going through what I was. I felt I could really help them because I had been right they were. It made me so sad to see others feeling lost and alone because I knew exactly what that felt like.

I had deleted my account from the online dating site and it felt good to do so. It had been so much fun being on there and I had learnt so much. In fact, it had been one of the biggest helps in me gaining my self-confidence back because getting messages like MILF and ones saying how they liked me and thought I looked amazing were life changing for me because I had thought no one would ever love me again, no one would ever find me attractive again and no one would ever want to have a long term relationship with me.

I had found a few Mr Right Nows, but I think I had now found my Mr Right.

Chapter 9 - Rows and Resilience

Sam and I were getting on so well. We were a couple in love and it did still come with challenges. We both had ex partners and both of us could relate to each other with the pitfalls. I was still feeling worried that Sam would cheat on me and this was a real fear of mine.

I needed lots of reassurance because I knew James had cheated on me goodness knows how many times and many I did not even know about. I was really worried I was going to get duped again.

I had to learn to accept that Sam had done nothing to make me think he would ever do anything like that but one of the biggest lightbulb moments was that I realised that I needed to carve a life that I didn't need Sam but one where I wanted to be with him. I didn't ever want to need anyone ever again.

Then if anything did happen, I knew I would be OK. My biggest fear was money. I never, ever wanted to be in the situation again where I was left with nothing and having to rebuild my life again because it had taken every ounce of strength to do that this time and I just didn't know if I had the strength in me to do it again. I was still reading lots of self-development books and in my car, I would have on lots of positivity.

One of my favourites was The Secret, which was all about the Law of Attraction. I would have it in the car and Harry would joke about who this Australian scam lady was. Grace and I would shout him down and when we went shopping, we would shout that we were using the Law of Attraction for a parking space and lo and behold, we would find one.

I wanted to teach my children positivity and resilience. There was so much guilt I still felt but by flipping the way I thought about it. I was starting to see that my children were more independent and resilient because of what we had gone through. It had been a positive experience for them.

They were so appreciative of the life we now were leading because even they could remember when we had no money at all and picking up pennies from the floor to give to me.

Holidays were what I would like to spend my money on because this was all about creating special memories. Things that I thought had mattered like owning my own home, suddenly seemed irrelevant. Flash cars and handbags just didn't interest me but seeing my children laughing and smiling and being happy was priceless.

They were both getting my bug for traveling and in the space of a few years, I had travelled to Singapore, South Africa, Cancun, Greece, Dubai, Spain, Portugal, Cyprus and New York.

How our lives had changed. James had never taken them on holiday since the last camping trip we had been on the week before he left. I was at the stage, though, where this no longer made me angry because I was still creating amazing special memories with my children and I knew I was going to treasure these forever.

Sam and I were finding it more and more difficult living apart because we were intertwining our lives together so much. I could not buy another house as my credit was still rubbish but where I lived, a much bigger house came up for rent.

I gently hinted at Sam about it to test the water and he looked at me and said, "Why don't we move in together". I was so scared at this point because I wanted to say yes but this was such a huge step.

Living with another man, my children would be spending more time with Sam than their own dad. Was this the right thing to do? Was I ready? I thought to myself was I ever going to be ready, but I would never know unless I actually tried, so before I could change my mind, I replied "Yes."

We contacted the estate agent and went to view the property and it was perfect. Just the right size for the four of us and then an extra bedroom for when Sam's children came to stay, but there was a problem. They needed a reference. I had bad credit so my reference, I knew, would be dreadful. My heart sank.

Three years later and I was still paying the cost of what happened to me with James. When we were alone, Sam reassured me that we would be fine. I showed them my bank statements and explained what had happened and Sam was right, we were fine.

We moved in just before Christmas and I went mad with the Christmas decorations. It looked like a grotto but somehow, I felt closer to my mum doing this as I knew she loved Christmas and felt like if she was still around she would be smiling down on me. Life was really starting to come together.

My business was in the top 20 in the company I was involved with in the whole of the U.K. and I was achieving so much and finally felt like I was going in the right direction.

We had a wonderful family Christmas and we were all so happy.

James was still being a bully and on one holiday we had in Portugal, I was doing a live video on social media as that's how I built my business and the next thing, he was commenting on it being really abusive.

I blocked him immediately and sent a message to him that I was disgusted that even years on that he was behaving like this. It seemed so strange that he was the one that had cheated and left me, yet he seemed to be the one that wanted to keep contact and pointing nasty comments to me all the time.

I just didn't understand it. I sat down and really thought about how I could manage this because I needed to think of something that would work for me.

Co-parenting was not working because although I was so much better than I was, I still felt like I was always having to defend myself against him. I read book after book and listened to seminar after seminar. In fact, I was becoming a bit of a psychology expert and was finding all this about human behaviour and personality disorders fascinating.

I decided that if I was to protect my mental health moving onwards, I needed to take action. I needed to minimise contact to protect myself because I was the main person looking after Grace and Harry. I realised that the constant abuse in person and via text was never going to let up.

If he wasn't going to change, then I needed to. I had no control over him behaving like this, so I needed to control what I could. I sent James a text to inform him that I was only going to communicate now via email unless he had the children.

I told him I was blocking him on text and when he picked the children up, I would unblock him in case of emergency. There, I had done it. I had sent it. I then blocked that number. I had given James my email, had given him instructions and it was time for me to start to step into my power and make clear boundaries.

I had tried for three long years to co-parent and it had been impossible so now I was going to parallel parent and still aim to do the best for my children, but I needed to protect my mental health as I could not spend the next 10 years with this permanent arguing going on. It was not healthy, and it was toxic. I felt nervous as I knew James would not like this.

For the last three years, I tried to be amicable and always try and do the best for the children and in response had always got a mouthful from James. Everything was my fault. Even our marriage breakup was my fault according to James. I was the reason he lied through our marriage, I was the reason he cheated through our marriage, it was all my fault.

I had suddenly realised that he was never, ever, ever going to be sorry. I could carry on like this month in and month out or I could take back my own control and step into my power. This did not mean he couldn't see Grace and Harry, it just meant that our communication moving forward had to change.

I sat and waited for what I knew would be an essay of an email, pointing out all the bad bits about me, and arguing about everything. Sure enough it arrived within an hour.

A lengthy email that I read and could feel my body physically react but this time. I was talking to myself saying, "Caroline, what is the point in responding to any of this? Nothing in this email is about the needs of our children, it is just an email to be nasty to me. What good will come from responding?"

All the knowledge I now had about how to react or not in this case was kicking in. I was in control over my reaction to this and the email had nothing relevant in, so I chose not to respond and react.

I ignored the email. I did not want to show James any emotion. My emotion always seemed to fuel him, and I was done with waiting for him to apologise. Waiting for him to say sorry and show remorse was like me drinking rat poison and expecting the rat to die. It was never going to happen.

I needed to take responsibility for my recovery. I was done with being a victim of my circumstances. Life was about learning and boy, had I learnt. I had learnt so much about human behaviour in these instances, so I was not going to give James any fuel to conflict with me. It takes two people to engage in an argument so if I didn't engage, then there was no argument.

It was as simple as that. All those years of trying to be nice, amicable and fair had got me absolutely nowhere other than to breakdown point. He was never going to change so I needed to change. It felt so good.

Finally, I felt like I was getting some control back and I was setting new boundaries for our parenting relationship moving forward. He could still contact me on email, but it was much easier to take your time to respond, and rather than a text where you get an immediate notification up, with email you can be more calculating. James did not like this one bit. I do not know how many times he tried to text because he was blocked but I hazard a guess of a few times.

My home-based business was going well. I was back in some

control with James and my relationship with Sam was getting better and better.

We loved living together and we were starting to carve out a life and talked about our hopes and dreams. Weekends alone were few and far between because James hardly had them overnight and then it had to also coincide with us not having Sam's daughters to.

But we found that the following month, we had a weekend where we were free from children, so Sam booked us into a hotel in London. We both loved the vibe of London and sightseeing and having long leisurely meals there.

Sam was acting a bit strange before we went. This always put me on edge as immediately there was any difference in mood from Sam, I seemed to absorb it and start to feel anxious. Was he having doubts? Did he not want to be with me anymore?

We said our goodbyes to Grace and Harry, packed our bags and headed to London. We spent the day sightseeing and had cocktails in Harrods in the afternoon. We had booked a Thai restaurant for the evening and we both got dressed up to go.

Sam was acting strange and it was making me feel really on edge. I had realised over the last few years that I was really susceptible to people's moods and I could walk into a room and tell you who was happy and sad simply by chatting to them. It seemed I could really pick up on people's energy which was great but in scenarios like this, I knew something wasn't quite right.

We went for a lovely Thai meal and afterwards, we were both tired and walked back to the hotel. We got ready for bed and cuddled and went to sleep. As I lay there listening to Sam breathe, I started to doubt Sam's feelings for me. I had never seen him act so strange and it was really making me nervous.

As I lay there next to him, tears started running down my face as I realised that I didn't want to be hurt again. I tried to rationalise that even if we split up, I would be O.K. now. I was financially secure, and I was able to take care of Harry and Grace and support the three of us. It was not as bad as last time. We would be fine.

In the morning when we woke up, Sam seemed edgy and nervous. We planned to go to Covent Garden for breakfast, so we got dressed and started to walk there. As we were walking past the statue of Eros, Sam stopped. He pulled me closer and looked in my eyes and said, "Caroline, I love you with all my heart, will you marry me?"

I couldn't quite believe what I had heard. Just a few hours ago, I was worried that Sam had gone off me when all along he was just nervous about asking me to marry him. He put a beautiful diamond ring on my finger. I had tears streaming down my face. I had thought I would never ever get married again as I had been so badly hurt but it just showed that with time and lots of work on myself, you could find true love and happiness again.

When we got home, we told all our family and planned a December wedding. Neither of us wanted anything large, just immediate family and a few friends. The day was wonderful, bringing two fractured families together and although we knew we were in for a bumpy ride as both had ex partners to carry on dealing with, both of our focus was on each other and making sure all the children felt happy, safe and secure.

We had a fantastic Christmas, although Sam and I had one sticking point. Sam wanted me to take his surname as I was obviously his wife now, but I wanted to stay the same as my children. I felt like Harry and Grace only truly had me as their security and I never wanted them to doubt that and they were still quite young.

I said we could have a double barrel, but quite rightly Sam did not want my ex-husbands surname. We did laugh that we should both change our surname to Starbucks but that was short lived. I just wanted my children to know that mummy may have married another man, but my most important role was being a mum to them.

Life was good, and James was actually now emailing me the dates each month. There was usually an essay attached but I just ignored it all and replied simply with the dates confirmed.

This was so hard at first because my habit was defending myself, but I realised if I was to protect myself, I needed to act like a boring, grey rock around him and that is exactly what I did. I became an expert at being a grey rock. Even when he came to pick them up, I would be polite, and he would often ignore me or on occasion he would try and start an argument, but I would just close the door.

There were hardly any overnight visits anyway now but when they were happening, the children were starting to get more and more agitated. I asked them what was wrong, and they said they didn't like their dad's wife. I tried to explain to them that she was their dad's wife and that they must treat her with respect.

I knew first-hand how hard the role of step mum was, but they explained to me how she spoke with them and they thought she was mean to them. As a mum, this is so hard to hear but I equally knew they also probably didn't want to hurt my feelings. I would try and explain that mummy wanted them to go down and have fun.

As much as I hated James, I totally wanted Harry and Grace to have a good relationship with their dad. It was really important to me. I did wonder if it was more important to me than it was to James?

James had asked to have Harry and Grace over Mother's Day weekend. Mothering Sunday was always a day filled with mixed emotions for me because I missed my mum desperately and never a day went by without me thinking about her but also, I was so grateful to have the best two children in the world. I thought about it and decided that if James was offering to spend time with them, because it was always so few and far between, I should definitely take it, so I said yes.

So, off they went on the Saturday morning, and again the night before and the morning, there were tears and lots of anxiety. I hoped that once they had gone, they would be fine and was so pleased they had each other. Their sibling bond had grown so much over the last three years and I know when they went down to stay at their dads, they both helped each other if one was missing me.

Sam and I made the most of the weekend and on the Sunday, I spent some time reflecting on my mum. I sat with tears down my face as I still could not believe that my mum wasn't around anymore. It was days like today that just reminded me so starkly as social media was filled with lots of Happy Mother's Day messages.

Myself and my sisters messaged each other, to say we were all thinking of mum and it was just so sad that she was no longer around. Sam had never met my mum, but I know my mum would have loved him. I missed seeing her bright eyes shining whenever she saw Grace and Harry and I missed her telling me how much Grace was like me.

She was like a mini-me. Just after 5pm, Sam and I were in our kitchen when the door opened and in came Grace and Harry. Grace looked upset and Harry blurted out, "Dad's having a baby".

What? Had I heard right? It stopped me in my tracks. Tracey

was pregnant? My children were to have a half-brother? My heart sank. This meant that my children would be inextricably linked forever to them.

Neither Harry or Grace seemed excited and then they got upset. Tracey was 6 months pregnant and they had only just told Harry and Grace. How dare they, I thought in my head.

Firstly, how dare they wait for 6 months to tell Grace and Harry as this totally excluded them and made them feel even more like they were left out and that their dad didn't care.

Secondly, why had James not emailed me to forewarn me so at least I could have been prepared myself? And lastly, the most evil. Why had they waited to tell Harry and Grace on Mother's Day, knowing how hard a day it is for me so that they come back home to inform me of that?

I chatted with Grace and Harry for a while to calm them down and they went off to watch television and I went upstairs to our ensuite. I started retching. How could he do that to me? What had I really ever done bad to him? Why would someone be so cruel and pick Mother's Day to tell your children, so they come back and say that to me?

Part of me wasn't surprised because I had become immune to all the emails as he was still incapable of setting an email with one point in.

But this? The cruelty, the calculating nature? It made me sick to the stomach. I was in shock and sat there crying for what seemed like ages. I knew one day they would have a family, but I suppose in the back of my mind, I always hoped it wouldn't happen. But it had, and we had all found out on Mother's Day.

I pulled myself together, went downstairs and Sam gave me a

big hug. I think this had even shocked him as to waiting 6 months to tell the children and then to tell them on Mother's Day. How cruel and nasty. Why would they choose that day more than any other day?

Was I just going crazy, it didn't make any sense? I think because all my emotion about my mum was there, I just thought it was so cruel. I went and ran a hot bubble bath and had a soak. I gave myself a good talking to and tried to move forward as no point dwelling on it as I couldn't now change what had happened and what was happening.

When I woke up in the morning, Harry and Grace said they didn't want to go down and stay at their dad's again. They both refused. Harry was really angry and was very vocal and Grace refused to go if Harry wasn't. What could I do? I tried to reason with them because I knew if I told James that, he would blame me.

I desperately tried to talk Harry and Grace round, but they were vehemently in agreement that they wanted to see their dad but not go down there anymore. I decided to wait a week before telling James because I thought maybe once the news had settled in, they would change their mind. But they didn't.

They were both so hurt that he had waited so long to tell them, and both thought James preferred his new family and that both of them were always bottom of the list. I told them that their dad loved them and yes, he should have told them sooner, but that didn't take a way that they were having a half-brother.

Neither were interested and it was just upsetting them more talking about it. I sat down and constructed an email to James. I knew I would get the blame and I was at the stage now where I did not care. I knew the truth and my children were now both old enough to exert their wishes, so I kept email to the point and said they will see you but unfortunately, they do not want to stay overnight for the time being. I tried to explain that I had tried but it obviously fell on deaf ears with James.

I got a blistering email back saying it was my fault. I was stopping them, they loved going down and that it was me telling them not to go. Little did they realise that I was the one trying to get them to go down.

James never once mentioned why they had waited 6 months. It couldn't have been due to worrying about the pregnancy because even I knew that after 12 weeks the risks of miscarriage dramatically drop so it was a mystery why they waited for 6 months and on Mother's Day?

So, the next overnight visit that came, James came up and just took Grace and Harry out for lunch. This became a habit and both children seemed really happy as they saw their dad and they came back smiling from these visits.

Once their daughter was born, James asked again if they would go down and however much I tried they both refused. Christmas drew closer and James was seeing them just before to give them their presents. The kids liked their time with their dad and were looking forward to having a Christmas treat with him.

I spent the day wrapping and preparing our family Christmas. 3pm came and no sign of the children? 4pm came and no sign? I tried calling James and got no answer. I was so worried. James always dropped them off early so this was unusual. It took me back to the time when James had said he had killed someone and all those horrible memories.

At just after 4pm, James and Harry came in and Harry burst into tears. What had happened? Harry and Grace had proceeded to tell me that they had driven down to Tracey's parents and met his daughter for the first time and had to have loads of pictures taken and pretend to be a happy family.

Harry said he undid his seatbelt on the motorway because their dad had not told them where they were going until they were almost there. He kept saying it was a surprise. Harry and Grace liked meeting their sister but just felt so pushed into seeing Tracey and her parents and felt really upset with their dad that he hadn't asked them if they wanted to go.

Harry was so angry at his dad and Grace said she hated it and didn't want to see Tracey and her family but did enjoy seeing her sister. I felt so sad for them both and so angry at James.

Why did he not understand that his children were of an age where they could fully see what he was doing and to think that one day of playing happy families would make it all better was insane. I cuddled Grace and Harry and even tried to explain why their dad may have done it. But they were adamant that he should not have done that.

The emotional distress they were both showing me really worried me as they were both usually such placid kids. The next day they had calmed down but said they never wanted to go down again and that I must tell their dad.

So again, I constructed an email to try and explain that I understood he wanted his daughter to have a relationship, but Harry and Grace were refusing to go down. Again, I got a barrage of abuse but this time it was like water off a duck's back.

I had to just keep focusing on doing what was right. I suggested he go away with Harry and Grace for a few days but because I suggested it, it was declined with anger. At least I knew I had tried though and left it at that. No point arguing as, again, it takes two argue and I was not prepared to fight anymore.

Day visits resumed, and it was actually much calmer now that James had to email. Every now and again, a nasty email would surface, but grey rock Caroline ignored and answered key points.

Over the coming weeks, I started to feel like I was getting lots of palpitations. I kept thinking that my anxiety seemed O.K but then why was I getting these? Some days, I would have over 70.

It started to worry me a bit as my mum had died of an aortic aneurysm, so I thought I best had to go to the doctors and get it checked out. So, the next day, I made an appointment and went to see him. I explained to him about my palpitations and said I didn't think it was anxiety but seemed odd to which he agreed.

He took me upstairs and performed an ECG on me. He studied it for a while and then said to me, "You have a prolonged QT". "What was that?" I asked, He went on to explain that it was part of the electrical heartbeat and between the Q and the T wave. I asked him what it was then and what was the treatment and prognosis, he just looked at me and said one word that made me shudder, "Death". What? Death?

Did I just hear right? I asked him to explain and he said that it was one of the most common forms of death in young people and age would be in my favour, but I needed to be referred to see a cardiologist. I was in shock! I thought he was just going to tell me to relax more.

Over the next month, I went to see my cardiologist who performed an ultrasound, MRI and I had full genetic testing. I even had to get Grace and Harry to have an ECG because if they found that they had a long QT, they would have to go on medication for life and cease playing any competitive sport ever. I was so scared because all those thoughts of not being there for my children came flooding back. I needed to be there for them.

Luckily, there were no signs of long QT on their ECGs. After all my testing, I returned to see my cardiologist who explained that I had a heart condition called Long QT Syndrome and that I was to make sure that my electrolytes were never out of balance and that I had to be really careful about any medication I took and that there was a list of medication I couldn't take. It was all so much to take in. This wasn't just a problem with my arm or leg, this was my heart, the consequences were death.

It really made re-evaluate so much and what was important and what wasn't. All the previous years of reading and watching seminars had now stood me in good stead because although I had just found out I had a heart condition, I now had a resilience toolkit to call upon to cope with hearing this.

My mental strength was so much stronger, and this was just a blip. It wasn't going to stop me living my life to the max because I had wasted so many years in my marriage that I had so much more I wanted to. The future was looking bright.

Chapter 10 - Being Your Authentic Self

I was working so hard on my home-based business and it was all going great. Sam had just started his business from home as a mortgage broker and life insurance advisor and he kept asking me to help build it with him.

He had seen how I had built my business and had predominantly used Facebook and I had learnt so much about business and networking. I was a big believer in investing in yourself by this stage.

That summer, we went on holiday to Cyprus with all five children. It cost us a small fortune but there was free food and drink on tap and happy children meant happy parents. Whilst we were on holiday, Sam asked me again if I would help him build his business and I just thought how can I get excited about life insurance?

It just didn't set my heart on fire and I thought how could I build a business around this? But I sat and thought about it. As I was lying in the sun, sipping a Pina Colada, the thought was not going away. He had sparked some interest in me talking about being online and branding.

I began to think that all mums should have protection and life insurance. I didn't have anything when I was going through my divorce and looking back, what if something had happened to me and I also knew that James didn't have any protection either.

 I knew it needed not to be expensive, so I thought maybe I could create a new brand? Maybe I could create something a little bit different and a bit sexy in this market? I could create a new business and network for Sam and this would bring him in the business of which I would own half.

I sat for a few days culminating an idea in my head and I found myself getting excited as it was a bit of a challenge. I told Sam my ideas and he thought they were great. A business that would reward people for staying healthy, save money and they'd have the peace of mind that they had life insurance. No brainer.

I started to formulate a business plan ready to put into action from the September after the school summer holidays and thought I would just take a back seat in my other business which was pretty much running itself by then. Who was this person?

Who was this Caroline that just four years previously had her house repossessed and £70,000 worth of debt? I almost wanted to laugh out loud because I had changed so much. I was not the person I used to be both physically and mentally.

I had worked so hard on myself and read, watched, listened and had been like a sponge creating an armour of positivity, strength and resilience. In that moment, I let so much go. I was good enough. I was worthy of love and success. I deserved to be happy and I deserved to live a life of meaning. I realised that the life I had now was so much better than the life I had once had.

I realised that I was truly grateful for all that had happened to me as it had taken me to where I was right now. I realised that had the trauma of the last few years not happened, I would not be where I was. The growth I had seen was because I had gone through what I had. Instead of the anger associated with my divorce, it was relief and gratitude.

I had gone from Post-Traumatic Stress Disorder to Post Traumatic Growth. I had read all about this phenomenon in my positive psychology text books. It was me! I had grown even more because of what happened.

Had my divorce not happened, I would not have grown so much. I thought this was such a positive way to see the last years events and I knew everything was just as it was meant to be.

I set to work to build our Life Insurance For Mums business attending network meetings, setting up our website and sharing with my friends the importance of getting life insurance. They loved the concept because they all knew they needed peace of mind should the unthinkable happen but to also get rewards was a bonus.

Sam was loving all the business and it was a great feeling to help other mums get that peace of mind. Sam was so good with the customers and we were a great team working together. It was so lovely in our house with Sam upstairs in his study and I was downstairs in mine.

Sam would often come downstairs and we would sit and have a cup of tea together. We were both at home and our marriage was just getting stronger and stronger. I joined a Female Mastermind Group called Female Success Network and loved being around other driven and motivated women.

This was something I was so passionate about because my

belief is that women should support women, not tear each other down. Just because one woman is successful, does not mean there is less success to go around.

I realised that a lot of female friends I had attracted in previous years were not the true friends I thought and took advantage of my good nature. This was a time to reflect on my own personal boundaries and who I wanted to be friends with and who I didn't. It is so important who you surround yourself with because you become like the five people you are around the most, so I knew I needed to choose wisely.

It made me realise that a lot of friends I had attracted in my life dating back to be a teenager all had very similar personality types. They always seemed to want to have something from me and I used to think I was such a doormat. I wasn't, I just did not have clear boundaries and people took advantage of that.

Life was good, and James and his outbursts were becoming less frequent as I either ignored them completely as they had no relevant content, or I just emailed very short responses. It had zero effect on me and both Harry and Grace were thriving.

Harry and Grace were seeing their dad two or three times a month for lunch and they had a much better relationship with him now. I was really pleased about this as it meant less drama before they went and after they came home.

Life was ticking along nicely, and I decided that I needed a new car as the Mini that I had was getting too small for my children since they were getting bigger now. I had the money to buy one, but I didn't know if I could get the credit to pay for it each month?

I had been tracking my credit since I had my house

repossessed where it shot down to the lowest of the low with very, very poor. It was now up in the highest level it could be, but I still had that fear that I would not get any credit and that I would look stupid.

Whenever money was mentioned or talked about, I still had that knot in my stomach as never wanted to go back to where I had been, and this was such a big driver for me.

So, one afternoon, Sam, Harry, Grace and I decided to go car shopping just to see what was out there. I had an idea of what I wanted which wasn't flash, but I knew they were good cars and a great size for my family.

We walked into our local garage and a car salesman approached us and greeted us. He was a lovely middle-aged man and was so helpful. He asked which car I liked, and I pointed to one in the showroom. He asked if I would like to test drive it.

My heart started pounding because I thought I won't be able to have it so is it best just to say no? But I thought it's only a test drive, so I said yes. We all got in the car with the salesman and off we went. I loved it and it was exactly what I was looking for. When we arrived back at the garage, the car salesman asked if I wanted to look at some figures. Figures, I thought. No harm in just seeing how much it would be a month. So, we sat down, and the salesman proceeded to break down the facts and figures if I had bought the car.

I knew I could afford all of it each month easily, but it was the credit that was making my heart race and my hands get clammy. The next thing I knew, he was asking me all these questions about where I lived, how much I earned and all my details. I was starting to feel sick.

Did I stop him now and say, "I am so sorry, but I won't be able to get credit because I had my house repossessed and lots of debt." Did I start telling him my sad story that I was consciously not trying to tell people anymore unless they needed to hear it.

What should I do? I looked across at Sam and he seemed oblivious and kept smiling at me. The further it went, the more sick I felt.

Then Sam asked the salesman who the credit was through. When he told Sam, I wanted to curl up and cry. It was the company with whom I had my house repossessed with.

I mouthed at Sam, "Forget it, then" and sat waiting for the car salesman to give me the bad news. He was so happy as he was thinking that he was going to get a car sale at the end of the day and I felt just dreadful. "That's all of it filled in so let's now press send," he said.

I sat there for what seemed like an eternity formulating in my head what I was going to say when the unthinkable happened. The salesman punched the air and said, "Good news, it has all gone through." I just sat there in disbelief and burst into tears. "Are you alright?" asked the salesman as I don't think he had ever seen a reaction quite like this before.

I went onto explain to him that I had lost everything including my home and that this was the very first thing to be in my name since my divorce. I couldn't believe it. I was back. I was now totally independent!

I know I was married but it was always so important for me to be financially independent and Sam used to laugh as he said that what was his was ours but what was mine was mine! I was so guarded with money, yet I would have given him my last penny. I just liked to see it in my account.

Having seen pence in my bank account years previously, I never wanted to return to those days. So, I had just bought a new car. I was so happy as it felt like yet another chapter ending and another new one opening.

I was now running two successful businesses, I was financially independent, and all was good. I had learned some great strategies in dealing with James and these were all paying off and I found I was helping more and more people going through a divorce and breakup, offering advice and tips to help them also move forward.

I loved seeing people grow and transform as I felt like I was truly making a difference. As the year continued and our Life Insurance For Mums business was exploding, I started to have a gnawing feeling inside. A feeling like I wasn't feeling fulfilled. I kept trying to push these feelings away because on paper it looked like I had it all.

Two businesses, a great marriage, happy children, but I felt like something was missing and I couldn't put my finger on it. I loved learning and over the years I had developed a huge interest in positive psychology. I loved the fact that this was all about what makes you happy and thrive.

Psychology was the study of what was wrong with people, whereas positive psychology looks at what makes people happy and what can we do to live a more thriving and flourishing life.

It was perfect for me and had hugely helped me in my own recovery and I found that as I was chatting to others I knew going through divorce that I could help and guide them using positive psychology. I started to look online to see if I could actually get a qualification in this and I found the University of East London had a Masters degree in Applied Positive Psychology and Coaching Psychology and was part time distance learning.

It was like the perfect course for me as I read all about it. Excited and nervous, I sent off my application and was accepted onto the course. It was so exciting, and my children thought it was hilarious that I was a student with a student card.

As I started my Masters, the first module was coaching, and I loved every single second. I had to find people to practice on and was absolutely buzzing after each session. I kept coming home and I kept saying to Sam how much I loved helping these people and that it felt so good. As the weeks progressed, I started to realise that I had a calling to help others.

The reason why I had been feeling empty was because although my home-based business and life insurance businesses were helping people, I wanted to make a real transformational difference in someone's life and I realised that everything I had been through the last 5 years had brought me to this moment in time.

But what kind of coaching could I do? I knew I could do business coaching as I had set up two businesses from scratch and turned one into a million-pound turnover within two years and the one with Sam was building huge momentum as well and I had built that, so it would run itself both on and offline.

But there were so many business coaches and was that making a real difference? Resilience Coach? I knew I could teach that because I had a toolkit brimming with resilience now but who, when and how? Then it was like a lightbulb moment that came to me and it gave me Goosebumps all over. Divorce coaching. Was there such a thing?

Did anyone ever coach anyone through a divorce? Imagine if I could help someone through the depths of darkness that I felt, and I could hold their hand through the process and help them redesign their life to be happier, stronger and more resilient.

My heart started racing. This was it! I got my laptop and looked online and I was so pleased to see that there was such a thing as divorce coaching. I went rushing into Sam with tears in my eyes and said, "I have found it. I have found exactly what I am meant to do for the rest of my life."

Sam looked at me and asked me what it was. I sat down and explained to him exactly what I was going to do. He agreed that it was all my passions rolled up into one as I love to empower women to be in control of their own lives and be happy.

All the growth I had from my own divorce and experiences had brought me exactly to here. I had been a counsellor, I had been a coach for 5 years in my home-based business, I was doing my Masters in Positive Psychology and Coaching Psychology, but I felt there was one thing missing.

Could I get an accreditation to be a divorce coach? I wanted people to take me seriously. I scoured online and there was nothing. It didn't really matter though because I was going to create my business and help other women thrive after their breakup. It was everything I loved to do with coaching, positive psychology and transformation.

I got really emotional then as I realised that the loss of my Mum, the debt, the depression, anxiety and self-harm, the repossession, the emotional abuse, my divorce to building myself back up and building two businesses, remarrying and being happy had led me to right now. All of that was all meant to happen to bring me to now.

I had to endure the pain, the heartache, the loneliness, the depths of despair, the dark thoughts, the having no money, the hating myself, the acrimony with James. It was all worth it. It was all worth it because I knew I could now go on and help others. I had been there.

I had been there and bought a million t-shirts. But I had not stayed there. I had worked on myself day in and day out. I had learnt what worked and what didn't. I had learnt how to heal myself and now it was my job to go out and create a business to help and heal others. It all gave me goose bumps because it just all felt like a jigsaw all slotting together to become whole again. I felt re-energised, I felt re-ignited and I felt ready.

Over the next few days, I put whiteboards up all over my study, writing all the things I wanted to do to create my business. I told a few close friends who all said that absolutely this was me. It was like a calling. I told my friends in my business mastermind group and they all thought it was an incredible idea and much needed as who doesn't know someone who has gone through a divorce.

I wanted to show the world that divorce does not need to define you and remove the negative connotations associated with it. Your life is not over going through a divorce, in fact it is the chance to totally redesign your life, so you can go on and live a happier, more whole and thriving one.

I totally believed this and wanted other women to feel the same. To stop telling themselves the same sad story but take responsibility for their life and not just live it but rock it. Then one day, I opened my inbox and it was literally the final piece to my jigsaw puzzle. The UK's first Divorce Coaching Accreditation Practitioner Programme.

This was my final piece. I would be one of the UK's very first accredited Divorce and Breakup Coaches. In that moment, I felt like my mum was watching down on me smiling and feeling proud.

She had brought me up to be independent, to be resilient, to believe that I could do and be anything I wanted, and I knew she was with me in spirit. So, I set to work to start to put things in progress to build my coaching business.

However, there was a thought that kept coming into my head and that was that I would never have been able to afford Divorce Coaching when I was going through my divorce. That when I needed help the most, I could not have afforded a coach.

This really concerned me because my mission was to help as many women as I could not just bounce back but bounce forward as I had and create a business to help as many as I could. So, I went back to my trusted online friend, Facebook, and I created a free and totally private Facebook group called Divorce and Breakup Support Group for Women.

To date I have nearly three thousand women from all around the world and all ages in there where I do free videos to help women heal and tips on recovery plus all the other women supporting each other so no one ever feels alone going through this process.

Friends for life are being made in the group. That was one of my main goals creating the group, that no woman should feel alone and broken like I felt. I had family and friends, but no one had been through what I had, and I truly believe that having gone through what I have makes me a better divorce and breakup coach.

I loved Facebook for this so I could connect on my business page, have a chat and then invite them to my group for ongoing support.

I also wanted to create online courses so that any woman when they were sat at home on their own struggling to move forward could go through one of my online courses and learn how to bounce forward with proven practical strategies.

I put them all on my website www.carolinestrawson.com as I wanted to help any woman from any other part of the world. I just loved technology because it meant that I could coach anyone, anywhere in the world if they had Wi-Fi. I did not want to leave the house when I was going through my divorce, so I know I would have loved a Facebook group and online courses to help me through this traumatic time.

Divorce is the second most traumatic life event you can go through second only to losing a loved one, so it is no wonder so many struggles to cope. As I sat getting excited and creating my business, I looked at other bespoke services that I could provide the women that I wanted to help by thinking about my own experiences.

One of them was High Conflict Middleman Messenger Service. All the back and forth texts that I had with James had really slowed down my healing radically. I felt like I was on the defensive all, row after row and it was exhausting.

I wanted to create a service where I would be the middleman and any messages came through me first from the ex-partner and then all the bullying, abuse or digging, I could eradicate and then I would just send my client what needed to be said and then I could reply with no emotion and to the point.

I imagined what it would have been like for me to not have to have had those endless text messages with James. Imagine how much faster I could have healed? This service alone would have been so beneficial to me. I also wanted to offer one to one coaching sessions either in person or on Skype and I also wanted to be there to help people beyond the coaching process, so I created my Paramedic Divorce Coaching Service.

This would be where I would coach someone for their session but then they could have unlimited text/WhatsApp access to me so that in those times where they needed someone, a quick text to me and I could help them dial down their emotions and this would keep my client moving forward. I loved this idea because I wanted to help see women through their whole transformation journey.

The thought of coaching a woman one day and have her leaving all positive but then to struggle a week later which may be weeks before our next session really concerned me. I wanted to be the friend that was their divorce coach and I could help them take the emotion out of the situation, not allowing them to keep telling their sad story and get them to reframe their view and move forward.

I was scribbling away on all my whiteboards in my study with all the services I wanted to offer and was feeling full of passion and purpose. I even thought maybe one day, I would like to create a membership to help women through the whole process, so they felt empowered with tools and never on their own.

I was soon on my course to obtain my accreditation and the course absolutely blew me away. I learnt so much and came away even more excited if that was possible. I just had such an armoury of tools now to help everyone. Just knowing that I was going to be making a difference in other women's lives was such a great feeling.

I also saw that there was a gap for affordable legal assistance through the divorce process, so I enrolled in a McKenzie Friend programme to learn how to empower others to represent themselves through the divorce process in England and Wales as the law is different elsewhere. It just meant that I could assist my clients with paperwork, filling in the forms and even attend court with them but save them a huge amount of money.

Divorce lawyers are not therapists and as such I didn't want my clients wasting money crying at the hands of a divorce lawyer. If we needed, we could buy single hours of time from a divorce lawyer, so this could keep a client's costs down.

I remembered all too well the cost of my own divorce which my dad helped me with and my ex-husband represented himself and if he could do it? I wanted to be a "one stop shop" for any woman going through a divorce, that they would think if someone had a friend going through a divorce that they would need to speak to me first.

I was so excited. It was all become real and I was going to be a Divorce Coach. I wanted to create weekend retreats at spa resorts and short breaks in a villa abroad where women could come and learn key strategies to move forward, but make new friends, relax and have fun.

All key aspects I felt for divorce recovery. I wanted to call them "Reframe & Rejuvenate" as reframing was a big part of my positive psychology. I wanted to put them all on my website so women could find hope and a new future all by looking on my website.

You can see the glass is half full or half empty but if you are focused on filling the jug of water up at the side by working on yourself, it doesn't matter whether you see the glass half full, half empty or even empty because you just pick the jug up and fill your glass. I wanted to help women fill their water jug. I had such big plans to help women totally thrive after their divorce. I wanted to be the light at the end of their dark tunnel and give them hope that it was all going to be OK. I wanted to be able to help women through a whole host of different aspects from should I stay or should I go, assisting with the legal aspect, overcoming heartbreak, betrayal and affairs, boundaries for the future, conflict and abuse, children and divorce, rebuilding confidence, learning to love again, getting back out dating with the perfect dating profile, creating a new future, being a Rockstar single parent to remarrying and blended families.

I had literally been through all of that and knew first-hand how tough it could be. But I had not stayed a victim of my circumstances but become a student of life.

I built my website www.carolinestrawson.com and wanted to write it from the heart. I didn't want it to be a stuffy corporate website where I was faceless, but I wanted to be real, true and authentic. I genuinely wanted other women to know that I truly cared and wanted them to heal, recover and move forward. I couldn't believe that it was all coming together.

That my dream, passion and purpose was going to be my business. I thought back to when I was a little girl and thought there was no way if anyone had asked me what I would like to be when I grew up, would I have said "a divorce coach".

But I was a big believer in fate. I wanted to give other women the hope that if I could get through this they could. That if you just take responsibility and reframe and refocus, you could live happily ever after divorce.

I could not believe that the woman I was now to who I was 5 years previously. James had no effect on me anymore and this was a feeling I never thought I would experience. It had all seemed so impossible at the start. I had felt so ashamed and lonely, that I was somehow damaged but not anymore.

It had taken all my strength to recover and I vowed to help as many others as I could to heal as well. Creating my business as an accredited divorce coach and positive psychology expert I believed would give me all the skillset to be the best I possibly could to help that person in front of me heal faster.

I wanted to inspire other women feeling at rock bottom that it may take time but if Caroline can, then I can. I wanted to go on that journey with them and see them through until one day they could turn around to me and say, "Caroline, you were right.

My divorce was the catalyst for change and I have completely redesigned my life and I am much happier now". It gave me goose bumps thinking that I was going to have this much of an impact on others because I desperately wanted people to feel unstuck in their current situation. What a five years it had been.

To think once I could not even look in the mirror, that I was using the corner of a toothpaste tube to make my legs bleed, that I had not wanted to leave the house, that I wore grey tracksuits and wore my hair in a ponytail, to having a huge amount of debt, to having my home repossessed and taken away, to feeling like there was no way out of a long dark tunnel emotionally, physically, mentally and financially to right here, right now.

Happier, thriving, flourishing, financially independent and on a mission to change the perception of divorce and being a single mum by empowering and coaching other women all around the world.

This is my goal from writing this book, to inspire and motivate because I have been in the darkest of places, feeling ashamed and lonely to stepping into the light and my own power.

I had a lovely home, with two gorgeous, happy and healthy children and I was with the man I loved because I wanted to be, not because I needed to be. I had carved out a brand-new life and it was even better than any life I could have ever imagined.

The thought of being in my marriage to James feeling sad, lonely and not knowing what was true or a reality was a distant memory.

I was never going to be in that place again. Divorce Became My Superpower and I am on a mission by writing this book to show you that Divorce Can Be Your Superpower.

Love Caroline xxxxxx